21/20.
8.40
745

CHRISTIE'S

Wine Companion

CHRISTIE'S

Wine Companion

Edited by
PATRICK MATTHEWS

With an Introduction by
MICHAEL BROADBENT

Webb & Bower
MICHAEL JOSEPH

Frontispiece
Cos d'Estournel, by Kevin
Jackson and Rima Farah.

First published in Great Britain 1987 by
Webb & Bower (Publishers) Limited
9 Colleton Crescent, Exeter, Devon EX2 4BY
in association with Michael Joseph Limited
27 Wright's Lane, London W8 5TZ
and Christie's Wine Publications,
8 King Street, St James's,
London SW1Y 6QT

Designed by Ron Pickless

Production by Nick Facer/Rob Kendrew

British Library Cataloguing in Publication Data

Christie's wine companion.
1. Wine and wine making
I. Matthews, Patrick
641.2'2   TP548

ISBN 0-86350-102-8

Typeset in Great Britain by P&M Typesetting Ltd,
Exeter, Devon

Printed and bound in Hong Kong by
Mandarin Offset

CONTENTS

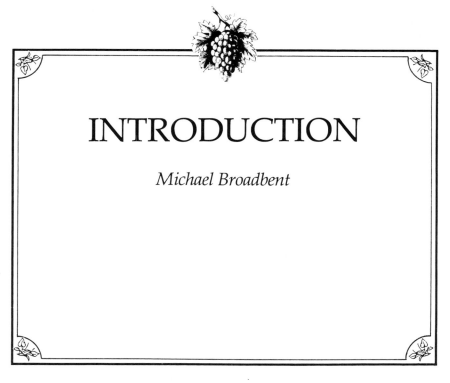

INTRODUCTION

Michael Broadbent

The new Companion bids you hearty welcome! We trust that between its covers you will find a rich variety of words and pictures, all in their own way paying homage to wine, wine areas and wine people.

This is not the first of Christie's Wine Companions: it is the third. The first, with a distinctive red and gold cover, appeared in 1981, and the blue and gold CWC2 in 1983. However, instead of hiding our light under a bushel, offering these – and other books on wine – exclusively to those on Christie's Wine Publications' list, we are aiming for a wider readership without materially changing the nature of the Companion.

In the autumn of 1981 I wrote 'the important thing now is that the vinous entertainment that has been put together will achieve what we have set out to achieve: to inform, to titillate, to instruct, to gratify the senses, to amuse, to make one ponder – but above all to please'. And to help encompass all these aims we have assembled a *premier cru* of writers and experts, all well known in their own fields.

Pamela Vandyke Price tempts us to visit the Douro; indeed, having read her contribution in typescript, galley and final paste-up, I cannot imagine anyone who has not visited the port-wine country failing to put it on their very next itinerary. If Pamela is indisputably the doyenne of English wine writers, Hugh Johnson is on his way to becoming doyen, if sheer professionalism, style and vast sales of his works on wine are anything to go by. Amongst the many attributes I admire in Hugh is his unsated curiosity. He is a great discoverer: this time, of Corsica. 'Watch out for these wines'; watch out for Oz Clarke, an opera singer by training and coloratura wine writer by profession, who has one of the newest and liveliest palates with a bravura pen to match.

I am particularly pleased that Don Ignacio Domecq – 'the nose' – was persuaded to contribute. A marvellous, modest man, whose office is next door to the tasting room which in turn backs on to the porter's lodge of that most distinguished of all sherry firms which bears his family name. Another 'aristo', Yuri Galitzine – we do not often have Princes writing for us – deals entertainingly with the history of wine, and other drinks, in Russia. Then, at random, Auberon Waugh, wickedly challenging as always, this time a trifle critical of burgundy; a subject more respectfully dealt with by Monsieur Bazin who tells us all about *Les Trois Glorieuses*. Simon Loftus, whose curiously named book, *Anatomy of the Wine Trade* established him immediately as a lively writer with an accurate and most discerning eye and hand as well as palate, gives us a pen portrait of a singular Italian vigneron: a complete contrast to the substantial and age-old Florentine empire of the still enterprising Antinori's, described by the American, Burton Anderson, who – lucky chap – has made Italy his home. And at home equally in London, Paris and New York is the man recently described as a peripatetic Peter Pan, the engaging Steven Spurrier (notorious in certain French circles for organising the 1976 and 1986 blind tastings of Bordeaux and California Cabernet-Sauvignons). Steven visits the wine fair in Orange via Burgundy: mouth watering and informative.

Canadian by birth, New Yorker by choice, Peter Meltzer analyses the American collector; Gerald Asher, English but immersed in the American wine trade for many years – and incidentally one of the most stylish of all wine writers – tells us about the courageous and successful wine makers of Oregon.

Nathan Chroman, the Edmund Penning-Rowsell of Los Angeles is critical of wine shows, of which he is a highly experienced judge, and E P-R himself traces the history of the first growths of Bordeaux.

James Halliday, lawyer, wine judge and wine maker deals authoritatively with the Australian wine scene, and Patrick Leigh Fermor, wielder of an elegant pen, gives us an affectionate insight into less rarified quaffing in Greece and the islands.

John Arlott, a warm and kindly man whose voice will always be associated by the English with cricket commentaries, is also a noted book collector and his wine library must now rank with the best anywhere: few more qualified to write about wine or books. Brian Beet is the sort of dealer who collects, or collector who deals. His knowledge of wine trade artifacts and collectors' pieces is without equal.

Helmut Becker's jovial countenance and tremendous sense of humour belies his solid professional background. It is the latter he displays in a piece about two great German oenologists. Dr. Skinner, affectionately known as Lou, has single handed made Coral Gables, Florida, the mecca for gourmets – he certainly knows more about food and wine than anyone of my acquaintance.

I started with a lady author, I end with one: Serena Sutcliffe, not only a Master of Wine in her own right but married to one, is certainly one of the most knowledgeable writers and best speakers on the subject. She opens the book with a Grand Tour Guide.

Well, there we are. All that remains is to thank Patrick Matthews, once again, for commissioning, selecting and editing another mouth-watering vinous collection, and to hope that you, the reader, enjoy the result of this, and other distinguished authors' labours.

Michael Broadbent
Christie's

GRAND TOUR GASTRONOMY

Serena Sutcliffe

Perhaps the modern equivalent of the Grand Tour is the Festival Route. The eighteenth century progress round Europe has been replaced by the twentieth century search for culture. For the Grand Tour was not essentially that – it was more often a useful *passe-temps* for young men of good family who did not quite know what to do. The sons of the aristocracy and landed gentry were used to 'kicking their heels' before inheriting, and foreign travel provided the opportunity of broadening the mind before the arduous task of minding a large estate or taking the family seat in Parliament became a reality. It is also true that during the eighteenth century it was not sinful to enjoy oneself. One could travel and actually revel in it, without the constraints of feeling that one was at the same time undergoing some form of forcible self-improvement, a blight of the nineteenth century.

Those who now sit assiduously in the front rows at festivals are usually older than the participants in the original Grand Tour. Maybe they are also more sybaritic, for our ancestors often endured considerable hardship in order to partake of what 'culture' was on offer. What air traffic controllers are to today's intrepid travellers, postillions were to the Grand Tourers. They both held (and, unfortunately, hold) a disproportionate amount of power and can make or mar a journey. The difference is that one could actually get to grips, verbally, with a recalcitrant postilion, whereas who has ever confronted face-to-face an air traffic controller? Travel was certainly less comfortable at the time of the Grand Tour (there are numerous accounts of the elements penetrating the flimsy curtain of a *carrosse*), but was it less frustrating? At least you could vent your feelings on postmasters and postilions, but the faceless adversary of a striking baggage-handler can produce sentiments of frustration.

Of course, the two Grand Tourers *par excellence* were Boswell and

Goethe. The effect of Italy, particularly, was dramatic on these two northern souls. They threw themselves into Italian life and culture, Goethe especially becoming positively abandoned in his uncritical passion for the country. They had the advantage over present travellers of staying far longer in the countries they visited giving time for all aspects of foreign life to seep into their consciousness. Goethe did not merely concentrate on the mainland: 'To have seen Italy without having seen Sicily is not to have seen Italy at all, for Sicily is the clue to everything.'

Boswell's Grand Tour included Italy, Corsica (not usually on any itinerary of those days), France, Germany and Switzerland and, of course, those fascinating meetings with the two arch-enemies, Voltaire and Rousseau. The Yale editions of the private papers of James Boswell give us the unexpurgated version, so licentious in character that it took 200 years to emerge. Certainly, the festival goers of today do not seem to have the sheer energy of a Boswell for combining appreciation of the arts with amorous pursuits. And it is doubtful whether their opera-going is as eventful as that of a Grand Tourer at the Paris opera – Samuel Smith and four friends shared a box, and although they compared both performance and opera house unfavourably with London's, they were visited in their box by a

Salzburg, where you can eat at the Weinhaus Moser, surrounded by *la toute Autriche (et la toute Allemagne, la toute Suisse etc.)'*

Mozart (1756–1791) was born in Salzburg and went on his first Grand Tour in 1763 with his sister and father. This statue is in Salzburg.

'courtesan' who afterwards was invited to their hotel! One somehow cannot imagine this happening in present-day Salzburg. The most racy activity in opera boxes these days is the surreptitious sipping of smuggled-in Krug!

Festival-going today is often accompanied by civilised eating and drinking in some of Europe's most compatible watering-holes. But the Grand Tourer's gastronomic experiences veered from the sublime to the frankly unpalatable. Good Protestants were naturally put out of countenance by *journées maigres*, with their restricted fare, but the rules were not always followed. Robert Wharton, who seems to have been particularly assiduous in cataloguing dishes, tells of a Lenten dinner in Paris consisting of soups, beef, roast mutton, fowls, pigeons, 'besides made dishes' – one hesitates to guess what these might have been.

For some, gastronomic prejudices seem to have been reinforced on these travels. Meat, of course, was generally not as good in France or Italy as in England (Robert Poole was particularly emphatic on this point), and oil was used too liberally in Italian cooking (Dr Swinton had a bad experience at Lerici). More strangely, for it seems to be the inverse today, the French were found to overcook their meat – both Poole and Tobias Smollett talk of meat 'done to rags'. One suspects this way of cooking was adopted to make the ubiquitous soup, much commented on by Grand Tourers. Ragoûts (variously and bizarrely spelled!) were on the whole regarded as suspicious, and the French preoccupation with frogs did not escape comment. Rome was a conservationist's nightmare, with porcupine, wren, hawk and woodpecker on the menu.

Some things have not changed – coffee is generally better on the Continent than in England, the French eat much more bread and salad than the English, Italian butter is unexciting, but the fruit and fish in Italy are of superb quality. Goethe said that Sicilian lettuce was delicious, 'very tender and tastes like milk'. What was encouraging about the Grand Tourers, as for many British this century, is the way travel broadened their gastronomic horizons. Dishes were tried, maybe at first with trepidation, but were often afterwards appreciated. Joseph Cradock liked a Dutch water-souchée, fish soup with tench or perch, served with black rye cake and 'hot India pickles'; Zachary Grey in a village near Antwerp fell for what was obviously the first winter salad he had tasted, a mixture of shredded

The Grand Tourer's gastronomic experiences would have veered from the sublime to the unpalatable.

The pleasure of a midday meal in Tuscany under the trees.

cabbage, grated apple and onion, dressed with salt, pepper and vinegar, while just about everybody went overboard for Italian truffles. Unfortunately for today's traveller, the best festivals generally fall outside the autumn truffle season, but supper after winter opera at La Scala can sometimes include these white gems.

There are all sorts of post-concert or -opera delights for contemporary cultural gastronomes: *bourride* on the Cours Mirabeau at Aix, perhaps after a gloriously-revived Handel opera (the ones they always said 'could never be done'); vitello tonnato on the Piazza Bra after an open air *Traviata* in the Verona Arena (Katia Ricciarelli, charming and pretty, supping with her 'claque' at the next table – but her Violetta was not Callas's, with the tigress's knowledge of the demi-monde essential to the role); or wienerschnitzel at the Weinhaus Moser in Salzburg, surrounded by *la toute Autriche (et la toute Allemagne, la toute Suisse*, etc).

Sometimes the gastronomic memories are more simple, and perhaps more indelibly printed on the memory for all that. There was rough bread, rougher chianti and gorgonzola, munched in the sun beneath Florence's San Miniato, before being carried away by a *Bolero* conducted by Paul Paray as if it were jazz (one *was* young and impressionable). And it was especially gratifying to stumble upon an amazing village opera festival at Martina Franca in Puglia. To add to its charms, the opera was Bellini's rarely

James Boswell, Grand
Tourer par excellence, in
the 'land of stones' drawn
by Thomas Rowlandson.

performed *I Capuleti e i Montecchi*, the orchestra was Rumanian (they all
looked like Nastase on a wild day), the singers were on loan from Naples'
San Carlo, and the mayor appeared after the start, following time-
honoured tradition and gaining much *figura* in the process. Here, pre- and
post-opera libations were copious *bicchieri* of the local white Martina Franca,
still or spumante, but always almondy and satisfying, somehow suited to
the slightly unreal nature of the occasion.

Boswell is maddeningly vague about the wines with which he was plied
by generous hosts, for the scale on which a Grand Tourer, equipped with
the necessary introductions, was entertained arouses envy today. But
when one is a guest at a court (and Boswell, in Germany, visited two
Brunswicks, two Anhalts, and two Badens, such was the number of these
independent states at the time), and the wines are served *en carafe*, it is no
doubt difficult to bombard one's princely host with questions as to the
provenance of his wine. At the table of the Prince of Anhalt-Dessau, 'half a
bottle of Rhenish was placed between two people – you might call for as
much more as you pleased', an admirable arrangement. Boswell continues:
'I shall not forget the luscious venison with currant jelly.' Nor will *I* forget
the splendid local venison served at the Gasthof Hirschen in a village in the
Bregenzerwald of the Austrian Vorarlberg. Here we repair after intoxicating
Schubert at Hohenems, where Peter Schreier has sung a *Winterreise* of such
piercing sadness that the spirits need lifting with more earthly matter. But
we drink Austrian Spätburgunder from the Wachau, one of the best Pinot
Noir wines encountered outside Burgundy, unfortunately a rarity and
dependent on really warm summers.

Boswell, writing to Rousseau from Lucca (ah, there is a small provincial
opera house to remember!) in 1765, sings the praises of his life in Siena: 'I
had excellent apartments at Siena. I ate well. The wine of the district was

very good, and on holidays I regaled myself with delicious Montepulciano.' Goethe, rather curiously, drank sweet Spanish wine in Rome aboard a ship which had just moored in the Tiber.

Eighteenth-century English visitors usually drank deep while on the Continent sometimes noticeably so. Adam Walker reports spending a sleepless night in Milan because of the high jinks of about a dozen English who drank 'thirty-six bottles of burgundy, claret, and champaign, (as our landlord showed us in his book) and made such a noise till six in the morning we could not sleep'. Who has not been woken at an ungodly hour by drunken revellers in the hotel corridor, maybe around the time of the Beaujolais Nouveau race? Champaign (or champain, according to the whim of the writer), both red and white, seems to have been universally appreciated. In 1730 in Vienna, Edward Mellish had 'drunk some excellent wine called Cotarote' and 'stayed a day extraordinary only to regale our palates with this delicious liquor.' Often have I felt tempted to do the same at the Beau Rivage at Condrieu, an excellent establishment possessing a fine list of Côte Rôtie vintages (here the spelling is all my own!). The usual 'sour' wines were encountered, and disappointments with wine drunk

Simple and unsophisticated, the traditional Italian cooking methods had changed little since the time of the Etruscans.

'upon the spot where it grows', but that is hardly surprising considering the relative frequency with which we met acetic or oxidised wines right up until the 1970s.

Perhaps it is the most modest repast that gives the greatest nostalgia. Thomas Watkins in 1788 wrote from Corfu: 'You will read it over a comfortable English breakfast, which is not however preferable to ours in the Greek Islands, of rich fruits, good bread, and excellent coffee.' Just south of Corfu, on the island of Paxos, I was writing the same thing nearly 200 years later, after breakfasting on warm bread collected that morning from the village baker, local thick honey, and equally thick black coffee brewed with its sediment and a dash of sugar in the traditional open, long-handled pot. Nothing much has changed, only the palates are different, but not, I think, less enthusiastic than those that went on the Grand Tour.

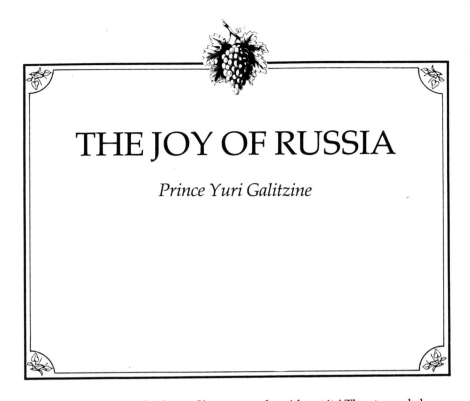

THE JOY OF RUSSIA

Prince Yuri Galitzine

'The joy of Russia is drinking. She cannot do without it.' These words by Vladimir, Grand Prince of Kiev, one of Russia's early rulers, who became a Christian in 988, are recorded in the Ancient Chronicles. They were his reaction to Islam, which he preferred as a religion until he found out that alcohol was forbidden to the faithful, but his thoughts describe so simply what was behind the Russian attitude to alcohol. For centuries strong drink was the only antidote to the vast emptiness of the country, the bitterly harsh winters, the dangers of attack and invasion and above all the squalor and the dirt.

Wine does not feature continually in the Russian scene; until comparatively recently Russia was a much smaller place than it is today and did not include the wine-growing districts of the south until only just over 200 years ago. Here the Greeks, when they founded cities on the Black Sea, brought with them the grape and the art of wine making.

The Christianity which Vladimir adopted came from Byzantium and each year the Grand Prince made a pilgrimage to the Imperial City. The Russians returned with gold, silk, spices and wine. No doubt they brought with them some of the civilised customs of the Great Empire. It was the Orthodox Church with its communion service that introduced wine to Russia and for centuries it remained a drink used only for ceremonial occasions.

In the first half of the eleventh century Kiev became one of the most prosperous and beautiful cities of Europe, larger than Paris and twice as large as London. The ruling house was linked by marriage with several other ruling houses: three daughters of the Grand Prince became Queens of Norway, Hungary and France respectively.

Until the advent of the railway all wine came to Russia by sea, either via the Baltic, the Arctic or the Black Sea. As long as Byzantium existed, wine

Banquet given by
Uncle Leon in 1903.

Wine List

Old Polish Vodka from
Pulsor

Livadia 1891 [1]

Koush Kaya 1885 [2]

Kaya Bashi 1884 [2]

Sparkling Galitzina 1884
Coronation Galitzina 1894
Chardonnay Sparkling
(Nature) 1898

Pinot-Herzenberg [3]
Troubetskoy 1886

White Galitzine [4]
Feodosia 1878

White Stephen from [5]
Sudak 1882

Riesling Massandra 1898 [6]
Pinot-Gris Trubetskoy 1899
Riesling Pilenko 1888

Livadia Cabernet 1891
Cabernet Galitzinskoye
1885
Morvedr Galitzinskv 1886

Saperavi Chavchavadze [7]
from Kvareli 1885
Saperavi Galitzina
(Feodosia) 1885
Saperavi Ai-Danil 1891 [8]
Muscat Novy Svet 1891 [9]
Fourmint Novy Svet 1896
Pinot-Gris Magarach 1834

Coronation Mead Emperor
Alexander III
Coronation Mead Emperor
Nicholas II

Muromskaya Spiced
Brandy 1874
Polish Spiced Brandy 1845
Vodka-marre [10]
Galitzinskaya 1884
Vodka-marre Saradjeva
1888

An outdoor fete in Maryna roscha (19th century).

was brought to the Black Sea by Greeks from Thessalonika, by Venetians and Genoese from Italy, by Frankish traders from France, and Jewish merchants from Spain. When the crusaders took and sacked the Imperial City the Baltic became the only source of supply for foreign trade, including wine. However, by then the centre of power had moved to Moscow.

In Moscow, the new capital, secular and religious life were closely intermingled, Byzantine survivals and influences being distinguishable even up to the end of the seventeenth century. Every national or court ceremony was primarily religious in form. They were elaborate and picturesque rituals and closed with ample banquets, but all inevitably involved partaking of the holy mead and the cup of the 'Mother of God'. To fill it, the communion wine came from France, mostly from the vineyards of Cahors. Toasts, however, were celebrated with red or white mead or with vodka.

Subsequent invasions by Mongols brought the destruction of Kiev and the whole of Russia became a battle field between the Russians, Poles, Cossacks and Tartar hordes from the East. The barbarians brought with them new eating and drinking habits, they taught Russians the pleasures of tea and introduced them to kumys, a mildly alcoholic drink which grew in popularity. It was said to be distilled from the milk of mares. Clarke, an English traveller in 1810, describes how his host gave it to him in a wooden bowl calling it 'vina' or brandy, but in the local Calmuck dialect 'rack' or 'racky'. Clarke considered it very weak, bad brandy, not unlike the product distilled in Sweden at that time. He tells us that kumys was made from

buttermilk, distilled and fermented over a fire made of cattle dung. Such primitive alcoholic beverages as mead, vodka or kumys were for many centuries the daily tipple of the country, for high and low alike. The mead referred to in literature will either have been kvass or hydromel. Kvass in Russia was distilled from a variety of fruit and is still very popular today; it is believed to have originated from the Greek Black Sea colonies, where it was made from mulberries and had a high alcoholic content. Now it is basically fermented barley flavoured with fruit. The 1914 Baedeker *Guide to Russia*, which gives a description of the local food and drink available, mentions three kind of kvass: Yablochni kvass (or cider), Grooshevoi kvass (or perry) and Malinivoi kvass (or raspberry). Cranberry was also a popular flavour. Baedeker also warns that foreign wines are dear, but that native wines from Bessarabia, Crimea and the Caucasus are 'good and cheap' – one rouble per flask (five roubles equals £1).

At table. A painting by V G Perov (1865).

An eighteenth-century recipe for kvass says:

'Take 35 lbs of sprouting barley, dried, 3 handfuls of rye, also dried, some unsifted rye flour.

'Put the whole into a big pot, add cold water, stir with a large wooden spoon until it becomes a light paste. The pot should only be filled up to about six or seven inches below the brim. Spread on top a layer of oatmeal, husks and oats, about an inch deep. Put the pot into a hot oven and keep it supplied with coal. Close oven. After 24 hours remove the pot, fill it with cold water and stir. Pour the contents of the pot into a larger wooden vessel

Elizabeth, Empress of Russia, drank kvass, small beer and an occasional glass of Tokay.

that is fitted with a tap and has straw spread on the bottom. Then add lukewarm water in quantity, depending upon how strong you wish the Kvass to be. Leave for an hour then draw off the liquid through the tap, pour into a cask and add a large piece of black bread to make it ferment. In summer the cask should be kept in the cellar, and in winter left for a night in a warm room, otherwise the liquid will not ferment. The quantities given above produce two hogs heads of Kvass.'

Street sellers of kvass, with little tanks on wheels, can be seen today dispensing their tankards on the streets of Moscow and Leningrad.

Another popular drink, relating more closely to the mead of medieval England, was hydromel, which was made from the sap of birch trees, honey and hops. This resinated mead sparkled and bubbled like champagne and tasted like a *doux mousseux*, so that many people preferred it to the more famous European wines. Perhaps it was from drinks like these that the Russians developed a sweet tooth in their choice of foreign wines in later years.

The Tartar invasions of Russia halted the development of Byzantium's civilising influence, and the country relapsed into a grey world of ignorance and superstition. Universal drunkeness was accepted as a matter of course, since heavy drinking was the only pastime of the nobility and banquets ended invariably in orgies.

When the invaders were finally driven out during his reign, Ivan the Terrible, a man of refined tastes, introduced meals of different courses, each with wine which was probably German, but mainly accompanied by mead or beer. However, Ivan's gastronomic attempts did not impress his nobility, who preferred to have everything on the table at once, so that they could grab food with their hands and wash it down with the nearest alcohol – wine, mead or spirit – until they collapsed in a drunken stupor.

By now, some wine was reaching the court from Hungary and Germany and a little from France, but only for the Tsar's table, or perhaps for those of his senior ministers. Towards the end of the sixteenth century the Tsar started to employ foreigners who were used to drinking wine in their own countries. By 1700 they numbered about 8,500. They were mainly in the army and prepared to pay the high price which wine cost in Moscow. As they grew in number they became a new influence in the introduction of western wines and western food habits to the Russian people.

Russia's conservative customs, however, ensured that for centuries the pleasures of wine drinking should be denied the majority. At table there was a rigid etiquette of precedence. One traveller in the late seventeenth century described how 'the best wines are placed at the top of the table, put in proportion as the guests are removed from the post of honour, the wine before them diminishing in quality, until at last it degenerates into a simple quas' [Kvass].

By the end of the sixteenth century the wine trade with France began to grow. The first great Russian embassy to France, led by Gabrilovich Kondyrev, left Archangel in May 1615 and met Louis XIII and his mother at Bordeaux. It was after this, under Richelieu, that gradually the export of French wines to Russia began to develop systematically.

With subsequent increased pressure from Europe to sell wine, the Tsars deemed it important to gain control of the situation and in the sixteenth century introduced a licensing system for wine and beer. This remained, until 1917, the Tsar's own perogative and brought in important revenues to the crown.

The accession of Peter the Great to the throne, followed by his trip to Europe, gave even more impetus to wine and spirit drinking than before, but eventually with some refinement. When Peter came to London in 1698, the capacity of the Russians for food and drink caused a sensation everywhere they went. It is recorded that on a journey to Portsmouth they stopped at Godalming for supper and thirteen of them consumed five ribs of beef weighing three stone, a sheep, three quarters of a lamb, a shoulder and a loin of veal, eight pullets and eight rabbits, and drank two and a half dozen bottles of burgundy, unlimited beer and had six quarts of mulled sack, before going to bed. Before starting off again next morning they began the day with three quarts of brandy.

Peter seemed to favour 'brandy'. In the memoirs of his general, Patrick Gordon, there are continual references to the Tsar offering him 'cups of brandy', particularly after dinner or church.

Alcoholic drinks began to feature frequently in the memoirs of Peter's reign. The Austrian mission to Moscow, for instance, in 1698 describes how their arrival in Moscow coincided with Maslania, the Russian carnival before Lent, when the whole populace was indulging in a drunken orgy and, the diary notes: 'Nor are the women more abstemious than the men. They are often the first to become raving mad with immoderate draughts of brandy; and are to be seen pallid, half naked and shameless in all the streets.'

It is here in this diary that we find the first reference to 'Florence wine' at the inaugural meeting of the delegation with their Russian hosts when the Tsar's health was drunk. At the first banquet they were served 'brandy, wine, mead of various kinds, beer and Guass'.

The meal commenced with 'an agate vessel, full of the most precious brandy' from which 'a tiny cup made from a ruby' was filled. The brandy was then handed round the top table and the meal ended with the Austrian envoy handing a cup of wine to each of the Russians present.

At the banquet for the envoy given by Tsar Peter on October 26 1698 the record says that 'the banquet was remarkable for costly and precious wines which the well stored cellar brought forth; for there was Tokay, red Buda, dry Spanish, Rhenish, red French, another as well as that they call Muscatel, a great variety of Hydromel and beer of various descriptions and that compliment which is not the least prized by the Muscovites – brandy (vinum adustum)'.

Wine was by then certainly reaching Peter's senior foreign soldiers. In the winter of 1698 General Lefort ordered 12,200 barrels of different kinds of wine from Archangel merchants, most of which was Spanish or Rhenish and apparently destined for 'the pleasure of the Tsar'. Peter never failed to find an excuse for a party, which inevitably involved heavy drinking. It was at the opening of the senate house that we first hear of a custom that persisted until the end of this last century, when each of the guests was presented with a large glass with a cover containing a bottle of wine, which everybody was obliged to drink down at one go. It was called the 'Double Eagle' from the imperial emblem on the cover. In the reign of Peter's widow, Catherine, the 'double eagle' was used as a punishment. It covered a pint bowl of brandy which had to be emptied by the offender who misbehaved at parties. From this, no doubt, developed the custom whereby each guest summoned to the court from a distance or bringing despatches was supplied with three bottles of wine at each meal. This practice, however, was stopped by Alexander III in an attempt to reduce court expenditure. But it is perhaps still reflected in the *charatchka*, where the guest has to drain a full glass of alcohol at a certain stage of a special drinking song sung by the host and his other guests, a custom which persists to this day.

Peter's drinking habits changed as he grew older, and this is reflected in

Pushkin seems to have drunk champagne with everything, especially foie gras and roast beef. (Painting by P Konchalovsky).

the instructions sent to the French court ahead of his visit to Versailles in 1717: '... He generally drinks light beer, and dark Vin de Nuits, without liquor. In the morning he drinks aniseed water (Kummel), liquors before meals, beer and wine in the afternoon, all of them fairly cold. He ... does not drink sweetened liquors at his meals.'

When in France Peter did not seem to find French wines to his taste, as he wrote to his wife Catherine, 'thanks for the Hungary wine, which here is a great rarity. There is only one bottle of Vodka left. I don't know what to do'.

It was in Peter's reign that fountains running with wine were introduced. Certainly this happened at the coronation of his consort, Catherine, and became a feature of large functions at the imperial court in the eighteenth century. Catherine I, however, was very conscious of the riotous behaviour which easily ensued at parties and laid down strict rules that 'no ladies are to get drunk on any pretence, nor shall gentlemen be drunk before nine'.

It is not surprising that when Peter's niece, Anna Ivanovna, succeeded in 1730 she frowned on heavy drinking and drunken orgies became very rare in her reign. Indeed, she restricted the amount of drink available at public engagements, except on the anniversary of her accession in January. On this occasion each guest was presented after dinner with a large glass holding more than a bottle of Hungary wine. They not only had to drink this down in one go, but often had to follow it with smaller ones. Nevertheless, Anna's court ladies still retained some filthy habits: they used to wash with a solution of resin in vodka and drink what was left over.

It was at the end of Peter's reign in 1724, through the good offices of the French minister, Campredon, that burgundy and champagne were first introduced to Russia. Delicate French wine soon became popular, especially Margaux, and under Elizabeth, who suceeded Anna Ivanovna, champagne took over from Tokay as the official toasting drink.

The Empress Elizabeth has been accused of intemperance but there is little evidence of this. Indeed, it was the influence of the German empresses, Anna and Elizabeth, that encouraged fine wines to take the place of the coarse old Russian beverages of kvass and hydromel at the court. Elizabeth herself drank kvass, small beer and an occasional glass of Tokay. Her courtiers, however, began spending vast sums of money, the benefit of which the wine industries of Europe enjoyed until the First World War. Count Razumovsky, Catherine the Great's field-marshal, for instance, ordered 100,000 bottles of French wine at one time, including 16,800 of the best champagne.

By the late eighteenth century the pleasures of the table had become a major preoccupation of the nobility. High society rapidly became westernised and assumed the elegance that persisted until 1914. There was a continually increasing demand for French luxury goods, wines, jewellery and, not unnaturally, at the same time the French reciprocated by developing a taste for caviar.

The French trade records for the period show the quick growth of the wine trade to Russia, for in 1756 the following are the export figures:

Brandy	255,000 livres
Liqueurs	150,000 livres
Burgundy and champagne	300,000 livres
Bordeaux	1,000,000 livres

With the conquest of the Crimea by Potemkin the way was open to the vineyards of the Black Sea. Production of table wine there at that time was primitive and quantities produced were small, but a variety of local liqueurs found their way to the cellars of the capital. In 1805 a traveller commented that 'the Greeks of the Archipelago chiefly produce wine of a poor sort, which is used in the distilleries'. The same writer, however, comments, 'since the districts of the vineyards suffered in the late hard winter the beckmiss [a sirop made from various fruits by boiling them with honey] has become more necessary. The spirit thus produced is sold all over the Empire as French brandy.'

As we move to the turn of the century, foreign influence grew apace at court. Many emigrés from France after the Revolution settled in St Petersburg and contributed to the refining of the palates of the nobility. French not only became the language of the court, but was used for day-to-day conversation in the home. The wars with Napoleon, far from affecting this trend, actually encouraged it. Indeed, Alexander I has been called the only true gourmet the Romanovs ever produced because of his love of French dishes and French wine.

Subsequent Tsars felt that Russian food stuffs, climate and customs did not adapt to continental standards so, food-wise, traditional fare remained the pattern of the Russian diet. This conservatism was to some extent reflected in the wines that the people drank. Centuries of drinking sweet flavoured drinks undoubtedly conditioned the Russian palate to favour the *doux* and the *demi-sec*, and fortified wines and liqueurs.

Madeira was a very popular drink in the early years of the nineteenth

Leaving a Kabak, or
tippling house.

Lukashka and Phytka.
Two Russian Boors who have just quitted
a Kabik or Tippling-House.

London. Published by Thomas Cadell, Strand, Nov.ʳ 1823.

century. It even reached the Decembrist exiles in Siberia and sustained
them through their ordeals. They were authorised for instance '2 bottles of
Madeira wine and 1 of fruit brandy', from which they were allowed 'two
small glasses a day'.

It is to Pushkin, Russia's greatest writer, that one can turn to identify
some of the popular vintages of the period. Champagne undoubtedly had
become the most popular drink of the nobility, led by the taste of the Tsars.
Memoirs of the time recall ... waiters in white gloves, blue and gold livery,
and red slippers, moving silently among the guests with trays laden with
food, champagne and drinks of all sorts'. Pushkin also mentions
'Tsimlyansky wine served between the meat and the blanc manger'.

Nicholas I, who was always very worried about his figure, drank mainly
champagne. One writer recalls him holding a glass of champagne in his
hand leaning against the red velvet curtains of his dressing room while he
discussed the regulations for a new prison. His son, Alexander II, is said to
have had a bottle of champagne every day to 'stimulate his languid facilities
whilst working into the small hours of the morning, as was his wont'.

Pushkin has many references to champagne, particularly to Clicquot, Moët and Ayala. Undoubtedly like all his contemporaries an addict, he scolds champagne as

> 'mistress-like, its brilliance vain,
> highly capricious and inane'.

Pushkin seems to have drunk champagne with everything. He particularly liked it with *foie gras* or with roast beef. Eighteen-eleven seems to have been a great year recalled in the lines:

> 'He arrives – the cork goes flying up
> Wine of the Comet fills the cup'.

But of all the memories of champagne, the immortal epic, *Eugêne Onegin*, contains the finest eulogy:

> 'From widow Clicquot and from Möet,
> and draught whose blessings are agreed,
> in frosted bottle, for the poet
> is brought to table at full speed.
> Bubbles like Hippocrene are spraying;
> once, with its foaming and its playing.'

Bordeaux was Pushkin's other favourite. He declares himself for Château Lafite – 'his faithful friend … a true companion to the end'.

The pattern of drinking was now set until the end of the Empire. The main meal was invariably in the evening and always started with *zakuski* or hor's d'oeuvres. With this there could be a selection of as many as fifteen or twenty different kinds of vodka; occasionally in Alexanders III's time *allasch* (Kummel) would also be included. Men who ate and drank a great deal often finished their *zakuski* with a glass of English ale. Then in some houses madeira and port were offered after the soup. White wine was served with fish, red wine with meat and malaga, muscat and Tokay with dessert. Champagne, as we have seen, was served with every course. At receptions in the Winter Palace huge blocks of ice, the size of small icebergs, were hollowed out to hold tubs containing bottles of champagne.

The annexation of the Caucasus had brought the wines of Georgia and Armenia on to the Russian scene. Much of this wine was rough, particularly the reds, and very unsophisticated as it was traditionally kept in buffalo, goat or sheep skins (with the hair on the inside). This presented the disagreeable appearance of carcasses swollen after lengthy immersion in water and was not improved by the flavour of tar from these bags when new.

Some superlative vintages, however, were produced by the Georgian nobility, such as Tsinondali from the estates of that name, originally belonging to the Chavchavadze family, which later became an Imperial domain. Other Georgian wines well thought of in 1914 were Mukusan and Napareuli. Tsinodali remains the leading white wine in Soviet Russia today.

The more sophisticated cognoscenti collected enormous cellars of fine wines, but by the middle of the last century chauvinistic pride led some of the richer landowners to develop wineries of quality on Russian soil. Two names stand out – Prince Leo Lvovitch Galitzine and Prince Vorontzow-Dashkov – both of whom had extensive vineyards in the Crimea. In 1851 Leo Galitzine introduced the champagne grape to Russia and his wine, Abrau-Durso, from his Crimean property, Novy Svet, became the favourite wine of the last Tsar, Nicholas II.

The Prince was internationally known, not only as a pioneer in the development of Russian wines but also as a judge of the finest wines. He was president of the international judges at the *Exposition des Vins* in Paris, in 1899. When he celebrated the fiftieth anniversary of the foundation of his winery he put an advertisement in major Russian newspapers inviting one and all to be his guests at Novy Svet. In 1912 he bequeathed his estate to the Tsar. The Novy Svet's cellars, hollowed out of the cliffs, extended about two miles along the Crimean coast. There was a hall carved out of the side of the mountain where Prince Galitzine used to invite his guests to sample his wines over lunch.

Wine production has now become a major industry in the USSR but since Gorbachev became head of state the consumption of all alcoholic drinks is being firmly discouraged. The old habit of the rich and poor alike, however, to seek solace in alcohol – dies hard.

PUTTING IT TOGETHER THE ECLECTIC WAY

Louis Skinner

There are so many approaches to food these days, with self-styled geniuses of the kitchen proclaiming their art as *cuisine classique*, new classic, *naturelle, minceur, nouvelle, pratique, spontanée* etc, that it is mind boggling, but just the same there is something to be learned from all of these schools of cooking. However, there is really only one way which can, at least partially, fill the bill for everyone and that is the eclectic approach, also encompassing the truant cooking of *cuisine buissonnière*; in effect an open season in the kitchen wherein no one branch of the cooking arts is used to the exclusion of all others, and the chef does his own thing. It involves taking a bit of training from here and there, using individual talent, imagination and creativity in modifying the ideas of others as well as building up a personal catholic range of culinary interests and tastes connoting open-mindedness and making use of whatever is considered best from various and diverse sources.

Eclecticism is a discipline. It can be readily applied as a way of life related, in particular, to the world of wine and food – an area where prejudice, one sidedness, and pure ignorance are all too common. The willingness to learn, try new things, develop new ideas and experience some of everything available, even if it is discarded at once or later, characterises this approach to the delights of the table – which is where I hitch my own gastronomic star. As we follow this epicurean culinary philosophy, let the chef follow his own creative fancies *à la buissonnière*, and at the same time we adhere to the fundamental belief attributed to both Escoffier, the famed international chef, and Curnonsky, the Parisian critic and gastronome, that *La bonne cuisine est celle où les choses ont le goût de ce qu'elles sont* (Good cooking is that in which things taste of what they are).

Good cooking aside, we should take a look at problems arising not from the home cook or restaurant chef *per se*, but from certain foods themselves

The Sense of Taste from the *Five Senses*. (Painting by Philipe Mercier 1689–1760).

that are irresponsibly used. There are quite a number of food lovers who, sooner or later, find out that they are intolerant or even allergic to certain foods. These are well known to the culinary cognoscenti as problem foods and they will screen and avoid them, never inflicting them on guests without knowing what their particular food hangups are. Known to cause indigestion in many people are brussel sprouts, termed by food critic, Iles Brody, some years ago 'those gaseous little half sisters of cabbages'. They have little place in an elegant dinner. Reserve them for your family and house guests who probably have similar tastes since sprouts, along with other farty foods such as cabbage and cassoulet, can be indigestible as well as socially repugnant. Care should be taken with cucumbers for, even if removed from an already made salad, they can cause burping just by contact with the other greens. Citrus peel, green peppers, raw onion, turnips, rutabagas and, most important, garlic, especially undercooked or raw, can cause symptoms of indigestion and even severe gastric upset. This treacherous and foul smelling relative of the splendid lily should be relegated to the farm for it is peasant food supreme. In my opinion there is no food that is improved by garlic – unless it is inedible or tainted with the early signs of spoilage. Heavy doses of garlic, and there doesn't seem to be such a thing as a little, would be better used in isolation at home where your friends – known garlic heads – can wallow in the stuff and insult each other's conversation with hideous blasts of sickening breath. Someone wrote an article in a medical journal about the lethal effect that garlic had on mosquitoes which bit people who had recently ingested large amounts of this insidious bulb. It was appropriately titled 'The Stink that Kills'.

Bearing in mind these problem foods, and the eclectic philosophy, we will take a recent menu and try to show how to put it together and achieve a memorable, well-orchestrated meal.

A mid-July luncheon in Miami honouring my two sisters on their departure for the cool of the mountains was occasion enough for me to invite twenty of their friends for a festive get-together. Being summer time there was obvious need to serve a light meal with appropriately small portions throughout and to have masterful light-handed preparation of the food from only the finest obtainable fresh ingredients. The courses would be accompanied by delicately composed sauces to complement the taste of things and not to mask or alter them completely. Likewise, light and cool hot weather wines were in order to harmonise with the food.

At the first one-hour meeting with the chef the whole menu and accompanying wines were discussed then tentatively selected. Only the test run remained and this was set for one week later – three days before the party. Fortunately, no changes had to be made except for some reduction in size of the portions, and the guests would be greeted with a summertime menu of attractive colourful courses each with its own individuality of aroma, texture and flavour.

I had decided to splurge and add a bit more festivity to the occasion with an appetiser of caviar. Fine Petrossian Beluga was served from the original tin over ice onto small crisp cracquettes spread thinly with just enough sour cream to hold safely a good-size dollop of the beautiful and precious grey-black sturgeon eggs. Nothing else was served that would obscure the delicate flavour. Certainly not the odious vulgarity of chopped onion or the trifling but too often seen grated egg yolks and whites which add nothing – only detract from the simple elegance of the caviar. To accompany it champagne, the obvious choice, was *de rigeur* as the French would say. Louis Roederer Brut was poured icy cold, at a temperature somewhat lower than usual since the glasses registered the eighty-five degrees outside heat of summertime Miami. This eloquent combination, speaking for itself, made as always a heavenly appetiser. Certainly one would not insult thirsty female guests by serving raw vodka with fine caviar, particularly out of doors at midday in July. It would cause excessive, disagreeable perspiring, and sweat is a vulgar word, particularly unattractive on the end of an elegant lady's nose. Likewise, taken neat, vodka can also induce numbing palatal shock – assaulting the delicate taste buds of the tongue and nullifying the delicate flavour of the caviar as well as intimidating the appreciation of other culinary pleasures lying ahead.

Things got off to a lively start and after a short half-hour of gregarious bubbly fun the ladies navigated the few steps from the pebbly patio to the air-conditioned comfort of the party room without anyone listing too far to starboard. Here, on the tables, the guests found their place cards and a little menu delineating the shape of possible muted gastronomic excesses with sensual winy overtones to come. Indeed, they faced a meal that would be interesting, exciting and different. This is how it looked.

A Mid-summer Luncheon
Vinton's, Coral Gables, Florida
July 25th, 1985

Champagne Brut (Louis Roederer)	Délice de la Mer Caspienne ***
Gewürztraminer 1981 Cuvée Emile Willm	Champignons Tout Paris en Gelée à la Ciboulette Sauce Quark ***
Puligny-Montrachet Les Combettes 1982 (Jos Drouhin)	Médaillons de Volaille aux Trois Moutardes Mousse de Foies Blonds Petites Légumes d'Eté ***
Château Coutet 1971 (Barsac)	Crêpes Fourées aux Abricots Sauce Apry ***
	Thé Oolong Formose Suprême

Délice de la Mer Caspienne was, of course, the appetiser just described but given an exotic sounding caption to stimulate curiosity and interest for the guests. The first course was a spicy delicate creation culled from a hot-off-the-press, new cookery book, *Cuisine Naturelle* by Anton Mosimann, the highly-praised Swiss chef at London's Dorchester Hotel. In thumbing through it with the luncheon chef we came upon the picture of an obviously light and different presentation of mushrooms called Terrine de Champignons Sauvages à la Ciboulette, but we changed the name slightly since we used different mushrooms. The recipe stated that there were several different types sliced and enrobed by a tender clear chicken stock jelly cut into the shape of a large individual mushroom. This delicately stylish aspic was enhanced by the flavours of chives and white wine vinegar which we added to the original instructions in order to make it a bit more exciting. The plate, neatly garnished with baby wild mushrooms contrasting with finely sliced slivers of bright red tomato and a sprig of envy green chives, was a pretty picture indeed. It was sauced with a lemon acidulated milk concoction, lightly seasoned and bland enough for its delicately sour pungency to contrast nicely with the tart spiciness of the fresh mushroom mould. We called this Sauce Quark, which was a modification of a Swiss-German item also taken from Mosimann's book – a type of fresh, low fat, low calory, soft curd cheese called quark. Our chef, René Madison of Vinton's in Coral Gables, altered this by subtle flavouring and dilution with *crème fraiche* in a blender to proper sauce consistency. This course was enthusiastically received by all the ladies as well it should have been, for they had devoured a distinctly light and piquant, smacky but elegant starter of virtually no calories, and what better way to start off a luncheon following caviar and champagne? The wine selected for this course was a spicy Spéciale Cuvée Emile Willm Gewürztraminer 1981 in the somewhat rare magnums. A beautiful picture they made as the waiters poured the wine from these extra tall, light green, Alsatian, flute-shaped bottles. The earthiness of the Gewürztraminer coupled beautifully with the woody taste of the mushrooms resting in their spicy bed of chives and white wine vinegar flavoured jelly. Likewise, the slight acidity of the food and the wine counterbalanced each other with the delicately pungent Sauce Quark blending in most comfortably. All in all it was a lovely course with a very complementary wine to accompany it.

So with appetites honed to a sharp edge, the second course could hardly be a let down and it wasn't. Two small juicy medallions of chicken breast lightly sautéed were surrounded by a fine lake of light creamy Pommery mustard sauce with its seeds offering a slightly grainy texture. This obviated any sense of sameness and ensured a good basic light mustard taste while contrasting softly with the two other more flavoury mustards. On top of one medallion was a smooth splash of orange mustard and on the other a splash of lime mustard; not enough to swamp the delicate chicken taste but enough to make it interesting and offer exciting flavour differences. The *coup de grâce* of this course was a divinely gossamer timbale of white chicken liver mousse in the Mionnay style of Alain Chapel. This ethereal creation was accompaniment enough, but three tiny pairs of colourful summer vegetables, zucchini, carrots, and halved baby tomatoes were sufficient further to make this plate an incredibly beautiful and delicious work of culinary art.

To accompany this dazzling dish a white burgundy – Puligny Montrachet Les Combettes 1982 from Joseph Drouhin – was chosen. With a good, full Chardonnay bouquet, it had flavour and body enough to hold its own, blending nicely with the savoury chicken breast and standing up to the trio of mustards, while not swamping the elegant mousse. Altogether, this combination made a delicious main course, not in the least heavy or dull. Interestingly enough, while talking about the food no one mentioned red wine, which I had thought might overpower the delicate flavours; also its temperature-elevating quality was undesirable in the summer heat. If it had come to red wine, for one reason or another, lightness would still be the order of the day. A pleasant Volnay, *premier cru* Monthelie or Santenay would do, or even a fresh Tavel or Lirac rosé might make the grade though I am quite sure, in my own mind, that the white burgundy was the correct choice. This course like the previous one was devoured to the last shred by the almost overwhelmed lady gourmet cooks present.

1954

"*Something in a nice white wine.*"

Desserts are often the most difficult part of a menu as the urge to cut calories involves severely restricting some of the mightiest offerings and concessions usually made to the ice cream bombe and cake set. Fruit is often the best solution if it is used properly – meaning not just raw fruit or grossly thick-crusted tarts and pies with more leaden pastry than filling. The imaginative modern chef should be able to come up with modification of or improvisations on well-known classic fruit desserts, making them both deliciously light and eye appealing even if he is not endowed with the innate blessing of creativity. Our dessert took the form of a visually enticing and finely made pair of small *crêpes* bursting with a lovely thick, unctuous purée of reddish-orange, flavoury Australian dried apricots, rolled lengthwise. Dusted lightly with a veil of powdered sugar and surrounded by a glistening pool of Crème Anglaise laced with Apry, Marie Brizard's fine apricot liqueur, it was pure bliss; and this smacky, scrumptious creation became even more heavenly when partnered with the mature, deep golden 1971 Barsac from Château Coutet. Its luscious but modulated sweetness, balanced with just enough acidity, assailed the fruity tang of the unsweetened apricots, making an exciting blend of flavours and sensual goodness on the palate as well as a visually stunning display of edible culinary colour.

To continue our eclectic approach and finalise this luncheon, a fine tea was thought to be more appropriate than coffee. A Formosa Oolong Suprême, with the delicate scent of peach blossoms which connoisseurs equate with high quality, was selected. With this fragrant Oolong, the personal choice of many experts and called by them 'the champagne of teas', this very elegant well-balanced and interesting, but not at all overwhelming, luncheon was over – though not in memory. Notes received later from every person present extolled the delights of the occasion, all saying that it was the most perfect luncheon they had ever experienced. In reality this was a simple exercise in menu-making with only three courses, plus the caviar appetiser and and only three white wines besides the champagne.

What made it succeed?

Following the overall culinary philosophy mentioned earlier:

1. A special occasion with compatible guests.
2. A suitable ambiance – pleasant surrounding, and enough space.
3. A competent, interested chef with a caring sense of respect for his raw materials and insistence on the finest obtainable.
4. Pleasant and efficient food and wine service.
5. Experience and desire to do something well be the host and the restaurant, with careful attention to detail.
6. An eclectic approach to the menu and wine selection plus interest in doing something different and exciting.
7. Keeping abreast of new things and ideas in the food and wine world plus the ability to improvise – taking old classics or someone else's ideas and improving on them.
8. Imagination, creativity, and knowledge of arranging and balancing menus, plus ability to complement them with proper wines.
9. Making the courses attractive and appetising while keeping the portions small and the calory content as low as is consistent with good flavour.
10. Insistence on a beautiful day when no one drinks too much, and there are no obvious upsets in the kitchen.

Above all, a slavish, over-serious, over-critical attitude towards the enjoyment and pure pleasure of food and wine is to be avoided at all costs since gastronomic myopia develops, all the fun goes out of it, one becomes mentally constipated and unable to enjoy any of the fine things of the table any more.

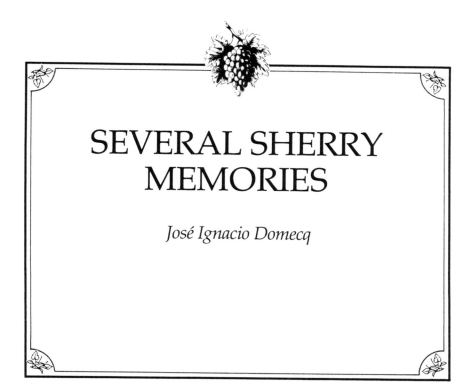

SEVERAL SHERRY MEMORIES

José Ignacio Domecq

With his characteristic flair, Michael Broadbent has kindly assigned me to write for Christie's a verbal blend that is easier for him to imagine than for me to realise, that is 'old sherries against a background of horses and grandees'. However, we live in an age in which pale cream sherry has been blended, with surprising success, and there is even something recent called 'mixer sherry', so perhaps I will surprise myself by achieving Michael's blithe assignment after a fashion.

First, though, I need to say that, while I coincide exactly with the outbreak of the First World War – and so was born simultaneously with what are now, I suppose, some elderly sherries – most of the horses I've owned have been only polo ponies. Although many of my relatives have gorgeous horses of exotic breeds, and various other friends and relations are grandees – or aspire to be – my own ponies and aspirations have always been plainer.

I am not in any sense of the word a grandee and I own ponies only in order to play polo, a sport I love. As we say in Spanish, *soy un hombre sencillo*, I'm a simple man. These then are my honest qualifications, and disqualifications, before I start on sherry, the wine that is closest to my heart. And to my much publicised nose.

And what better starting point for sherry memories than the nose? Growing up in and around the sherry *bodegas* of one's family must be one of the most deliciously fragrant childhoods on this planet.

Today I read in American magazines that makers of perfumes refer to their business as 'the fragrance industry'. Also there are essence makers who can reproduce flavours and fragrances of every sort in their laboratories, for incorporation into products that are eventually sold as rich-and-rare old such-and-such, when their reality is sadly otherwise. But I digress. Back in the antediluvian days of my Jerez childhood the world was

José Ignacio Domecq blending in the sample room next to his office.

an innocent place, and the blended scents of our *bodegas* were then – as they still are today – the honest co-mingling of oak and wine in vast shaded spaces, like whitewashed cathedrals, under the Andalusian sun.

As far back as I can remember, my organoleptic memory has filed away sherry aromas, running the gamut from the fresh pressed must of *palomino* grapes to olorosos dating back to 1730, the year of our firm's foundation ... (and, incidentally, the birth year of James Christie, which coincidence Domecq and Christie's co-celebrated in 1980 with a Tres Cortados I was honoured to blend for the occasion).

Mention of blending prompts me now to state a fact that will be familiar to most of the *Wine Companion*'s readers: simply that sherry, unlike quality table wines, is almost always blended. Our *solera* system of educating young wines via exposure to their elders is already a kind of blending process. But then further blends are made to match each company's criteria. Thereby, La Ina, for instance, my own firm's premium fino, is easily distinguished from other finos by characteristics we believe make it 'the world's most civilised aperitif'. (Some years ago we advertised 'La Ina is like a beautiful woman'; also that 'Sherry is Domecq'. All such slogans appear and disappear as advertising agencies are changed, but happily the wine goes on the same, regardless.)

Perhaps that is one of the most gratifying aspects of having spent one's life in ancient *bodegas*. One watches human egos come and go – all talking loudly about market trends etc, in the jargon of the moment – while the wine ignores them all and silently ages, turning itself with our tactful guidance into the same lovely old perfection enjoyed by our ancestors.

Enjoyment of sherry by my own ancestors is putting it mildly. I think nowhere in the wine world have I witnessed such whole-hearted devotion to their own wine's consumption as that of my family here in Jerez. Not now, of course – current Domecqs are relatively abstemious – but in the days of my uncle, José Domecq Villavicencio … In those days it was still not uncommon to age separately a specific vintage if the wine was deemed something special. Twenty-two butts of the 1918 vintage turned out as exceptional oloroso, so were stored in their own little niche in a dark corner of El Molino *bodega*. Nine years later my father was planning a blend for London and decided this 1918 oloroso was precisely the wine to include for its richness. After an entire day's searching, the twenty-two butts were still invisible. Losing his temper at last, he shouted at one deaf old foreman, 'Where the devil have you put that 1918 oloroso from so-and-so vineyard?' 'I haven't put it anywhere. Your brother, Don José, drank the lot', was the simple answer. Twenty-two butts is approximately 11,000 litres! However, my Uncle José was a generous man with many friends. And, obviously, they all appreciated fine oloroso.

Fortunately, I've been able to safeguard more carefully my own inheritance of old oloroso. It's a small, personal – and to me very precious –

Henry Ford II had an unusual style with the *venencia*.

cache set aside by my father. Every now and then I have a dozen bottles filled and labelled MDV, my father's initials (Manuel Domecq Villavicencio). Over seventy-five years old on average, even a single *copita* of this wine will soon fill a fair-sized room with its bouquet, the centuries-old scent of a sherry *bodega*.

If I look at MDV or one of our other much older wines in the sample room attached to my office, next door to El Molino, I then have to abandon examining young wines for the rest of the morning. The atmosphere is just too saturated by enormous old aromas for fine judgment of delicate

'Someone said this reminds them of Don Quixote riding out to joust with the windmill.'

Opposite
'To sip a *copita* of fino, fresh and cool from the butt, is more pleasant than you would suppose from my stern expression'.

DOMECQ OBLIGE

The family coat-of-arms.

nuances. So, in practice, I usually nose the old wines *in situ*, via my *venencia* – the whalebone-shafted, silver-cupped dipper we use in Jerez – straight from cask in the *bodega*.

Strolling through a *bodega*, dipping out old sherries which have rested undisturbed for generations, must be one of the most satisfying encounters a man can have with wine. At moments in my life when some insoluble problem has weighed on my mind I have unhooked my father's old *venencia* from behind the door and browsed through a few ancient sherries next door. Maybe the problem is still insoluble, but by nosing and sipping a bit of history I see my position in better perspective.

Wine Companion readers will realise that these old sherries fall into three types: amontillado, oloroso, and palo cortado, since fino is not a wine for ageing, unless it's one of those finos destined to become an amontillado. The evolution of some finos into amontillados – by a natural process we can't control – is, I believe, sherry's second mystery. The first mystery is surely how new wine will eventually decide for itself, again, beyond our control, whether it will evolve as oloroso or fino. Similarly mysterious are such 'sacred monster' sherries as those we still hold in El Molino from 1730. Concentrated by a quarter-millenium, their aroma is so overpowering that it's virtually impossible to distinguish between an oloroso and a palo cortado. An extremely old amontillado is easier to identify, especially on the palate, by its lighter body.

Although Michael Broadbent suggested I write on *old* sherries I'll take the liberty of praising some of the present generation, that is to say sherries matured within the last twenty years. In particular I'd like to mention such a rarely true bone-dry oloroso as our own Rio Viejo, the almost inevitable prelude in my family to fino La Ina. By generally accepted Domecq custom, our first *copita* or two of the day will almost always be Rio Viejo. Then most men go on to very cold La Ina, while many women continue to sip dry oloroso. Some outsiders are surprised to find that we usually chill an oloroso; not as cold as a fino, but definitely cool. Just enough to refresh the mouth, without loss to nose or palate.

Whether shooting partridge in the vineyards, sailing on Cádiz Bay, or after polo, most groups are armed with at least two huge thermos bottles of chilled wine – Rio Viejo and La Ina – for which nice old leather double-barrelled thermos carriers still exist; wonderful relics with their red baize linings. To go with these, some of us cherish well-worn leather cases, formerly made by local Jerez saddlers, each small case containing a built-in nest of six two-centilitre shotglasses; perfect for the sharing of sherry at sporting events. I have innocently aroused some interest in England at point-to-points or polo by producing such family sherry paraphernalia.

At last, then, I come to polo ponies, about which I really have little to say, since the proof of ponies is in their riding. I suppose, in well over fifty years of polo, I've known thousands of these splendid creatures. Some were better and some were worse. Basically, a good pony needs speed, stamina, courage, balance, and the right temperament; neither too excitable nor too lethargic.

Thus described, that still leaves grandees, to end my assignment. Well, I suppose grandees might also answer the above description. Indeed, why not? Certainly they tend to be rather splendid creatures. And – like the rest of us – some are better and some are worse.

Unlike good sherry – if I may say so – which is almost always even better than one expects.

BURGUNDY NOW AND THEN

Auberon Waugh

I wonder if I am alone among serious wine buyers and drinkers in suspecting that there is a conspiracy in the trade, aided and abetted by wine writers and 'experts' with wine connections, to bully us into buying whatever they have to sell. If such a conspiracy exists, it is almost certainly unspoken and might even flourish beneath the conscious awareness of the conspirators. Nor is it confined to burgundy. My first mistake was to be taken in by all the hype for the 1975 vintage port. I bought cases and cases on expert assurances that it would be the vintage of the century. When the 1977 vintage came round, I initially felt that the trade had called 'wolf' once too often, and so had to buy what undoubtedly will prove to be a major vintage much more expensively later on. Where claret is concerned, I observe with amazement that Alexis Lichine, in the new edition of his *Encyclopaedia of Wines and Spirits* (Cassell), awards the 1984 vintage seventeen out of a possible twenty points – exactly the same high score as he awards to such excellent vintages as 1959 and 1971. Now I have not tasted any of the 1984 red bordeaux yet, and I suppose it is possible that Mr Lichine may be right. But I am also aware that 1984 marked the virtual failure of the *merlot* grape, that wines will be thrown out of their traditional balance as a result, and that other experts, who *have* tasted the wines and are not connected with the trade, have discussed the vintage in terms of another 1972, which will burst the claret price bubble yet again. But of course the trade must sell these 1984 red bordeaux somehow. Private wine buyers (not to mention business expansion schemes) will not find out their mistake, if it is a mistake, for at least five years, by which time some really good vintages will have come along which people will be queueing up to buy at any price they ask.

Where burgundy is concerned, the conspiracy may have gone even further. I was touched and moved to read in a new book by Don Hewitson, the extrovert New Zealander (*Enjoying Wine*, Elm Tree Books), that he has had exactly the same experience as I have. Writing about his memories of the 1960s, he says 'there were the unparalleled joys of enjoying reasonably priced attractive, rich and luscious burgundies. A dinner time bottle of commonplace Côte de Beaune-Villages would ease the worries of the business day: now all a similar bottle does is make me annoyed (at the thinness and lack of fruit) and resentful (if I have paid out sufficient money to buy a couple of bottles of excellent claret or Beaujolais).'

One explanation could be that Hewitson and I have faulty memories – that it is not the product which has changed, but our capacity to enjoy it. However, as a third 'jilted lover of red burgundy' – Howard Ripley – points out, it is still possible to find exactly the same wine as we remember, here and there, although neither the year, nor the commune, nor the vineyard shown on the label provide sufficient guidance to identify such wines. A famous lady wine expert – who certainly knows twenty times as much as I do on the subject – told me at lunch recently that what she especially enjoyed about burgundy was identifying the particular character of each commune – whether Volnay, Chambolle, Santenay or what you will – and then proceeding to guess the vineyard. My own experience of the wine suggests that this is an absurdity. Not only do the communes have no identifiable characteristics – in the sense that the range of wines in each is too big to make any generalisations useful – but even within one vineyard, frequently shared between twenty or thirty growers, you get vines of all ages, some well pruned and producing a beautiful, rich intense wine which might have come from a *grand cru* of the 1950s, others unpruned, over-fertilised and producing a pale, thin red wine smelling of raw meat which might have come from Sancerre on the Loire. In a big *climat* like Clos de Vougeot, shared between over a hundred growers, many producing their own wine in their own way, and with a huge variety of sub-soils in a tiny area, it is possible to find wines of the same year coming from adjoining patches of land which are as different as chalk from cheese.

The result is that it is almost impossible to be knowledgeable about burgundy. While it is comparatively easy to learn about the *châteaux* and vintages of Bordeaux, there is no equivalent store of knowledge to be had about the myriad growers of Burgundy. As Anthony Hanson makes plain in his authoritative treatise, *Burgundy* (Faber and Faber, 1982): 'There is absolutely no substitute for tasting what is in the bottle.'

Mr Hanson knows as much about burgundy as any man alive. He certainly knows twenty times as much as I do, just as Mr Alexis Lichine knows about a hundred times as much as I do about claret, which did not prevent him from awarding the 1984 bordeaux seventeen points out of twenty. In fact it added to his authority in making this assessment. The fact that Mr Hanson may be connected with the trade did not prevent him from publishing one of the savagest attacks on declining standards in the area which I have ever read, when he wrote about 'mediocre wines without quality and poor value for money. Briefly, a rip-off. The Burgundians are coasting along on their reputation.' This judgement was endorsed by David Wolfe after a recent tasting of Gevrey Chambertins, where he decided there was not a single wine on offer which he would have bought: 'The general malaise of Burgundy may be summed up as a startling disparity between quality and price.' In other words, the limited quantity of red wine which

One of those Burgundian underground cellars – very cold in winter.

Burgundy can produce – I do not propose to discuss white burgundy in this piece, since it is an entirely different subject – is so over-subscribed as a result of people's memories of how burgundy used to taste that the growers can sell their products no matter how silly and thin they taste now.

My point is that Mr Hanson is plainly an honest man, just as Mr Lichine is plainly an honest man. Mr Hanson is also someone who has to sell whatever burgundy he can buy, having decided that it is the best on offer. In the present circumstances of the wine trade this means that he has to sell it as soon as it comes in – possibly two or three years after the grapes are gathered and pressed. From my memory of twenty-five to thirty years ago, one was practically never offered respectable burgundy before it was at least six years in bottle. The pressure on wine growers to produce quick-maturing wine, drinkable after two or three years, has never been greater, but in fact no process has yet been discovered which will have the same effect on wine as ageing in bottle. If the growers can sell their wine without ageing it there is no reason for them to age it; if the wine merchants are unable to age their wine as a result of financial constrictions, they must somehow persuade the public to buy immature wine and pretend it is ready for drinking, since very few wine drinkers have either the space or the patience to lay down wine for eight or nine years (let alone the twenty-five or so years needed by some of the best clarets and ports) and in many cases they may be doubtful of the necessary life expectancy.

The conspiracy within the wine trade thus takes two forms: on growers

to produce dilute wines in large quantities, insufficiently vatted, to make quick and easy drinking; and on merchants to pretend at the same time that these thin, pale burgundies are what the wine should really taste like, or alternatively (now the consumers are getting wise to this trick), that burgundies made properly according to the instructions of Napoleon's Minister of Agriculture, Jean Chaptal, in 1801 – he is the father of what is now called traditional burgundy – may be drunk within a few years of vintage.

Chaptal's instructions, as Mr Hanson pointed out in his learned and informative article 'Burgundy then and now' in an earlier edition of *Christie's Wine Companion*, permitted the addition of sugar and boiling must and prescribed a weighted cover on floating grape skins in the vat to allow maximum infusion of tannin – the recipe for a slow-maturing wine of great density. They were also interpreted to allow the 'beefing up' of thin vintages by addition of coarse young Rhône and Midi wines and, for the English market, brandy and even port.

Obviously such blending or 'beefing up' required enormous skill. Over-sugaring produced a wine which was either too alcoholic or too sweet, over-vatting produced a wine which was excessively raw and tannic, overblending produced a wine which lacked any of the characteristic excellences or subtlety of the *pinot* grape. The extent to which these practices are now regarded as heretical – some of them are even illegal – is illustrated by the way that the word 'chaptalised', deriving from

The hill of Corton north of Beaune which bears grapes for red wine at the eastern end and for white at the western.

"You mean France makes burgundy, too?"

Napoleon's blameless Minister of Agriculture, is now used almost exclusively to denote a wine which has been over-sugared or over-cooked. Yet it was these practices which produced, year after year, the splendid wines which Don Hewitson remembers, wines which can still be found at auction, usually in English bottlings by Berry Bros, Averys of Bristol or British Rail. The best ones need ten to fifteen years in bottle and lived for anything up to another ten years after that.

Mr Hanson, in his chapter in *Christie's Wine Companion*, mentioned that for the first 1,350 years or so of its existence as a wine-producing area, Burgundy produced a light, fast-maturing wine. It was only in the nineteenth century that longer vatting time and Mr Chaptal's other remedies started producing the deep, intense wines we grew to know and love in England. He suggests that this English taste may be some form of perversion, like our national taste for being whipped. I remember once, in a flight of fancy, describing a burgundy I was offering to members of the

Spectator Wine Club, which I organise, as 'anal'. Left-wingers and progressives will be delighted to learn that it was a sell-out.

But the argument that early practices must hold some greater validity than those which emerged from the wonderful cauldron of intellectual and scientific discovery which was the nineteenth century simply won't do. One hears the same arguments advanced in liturgical discussion: that the early Christians always used to play guitars, embrace each other and share buns together at their impromptu love-feasts which preceded the formalised ceremonies of eucharist or mass. It is all a load of rubbish. Tradition and conservatism are bound to embrace whatever is useful in the process of change or development, as well as fighting the good fight against harmful change. I can well understand that it would be much more convenient for the wine trade if we could be persuaded to accept burgundy as a light, fast-maturing wine. But consumers must learn to resist this suggestion and stamp on it whenever it is made. Wine merchants should be joining the battle on their behalf against the growers and producers, not taking their side. If a tiny proportion of the Common Agricultural Policy funds paid to wine makers in the Midi for producing millions of gallons of undrinkable wine for the wine lake was devoted to encouraging serious producers to age their wine before sale, the world would be a happier and saner place.

One began to suspect that Mr Hanson was arguing a case rather than writing from the heart when he started quoting ancient authors in his attempt to prove that burgundy was and should be a light, quick-maturing wine. Being an honest man, he also supplied us with all the ammunition needed to knock down his arguments: thus the reason burgundy was formerly a paler wine was not over-production, as now, but that a large proportion of white grapes was included. When he quoted Cyrus Redding, in 1851, as reckoning that a bottle of burgundy peaked after two years, he also recorded Mr Redding's impression that Chambolle was in the Côte de Beaune, Vosne and Romanée in the Côte Chalonaise, adding weakly that Mr Redding at least gave the impression of having gathered his facts at first hand. I am surprised that he did not pick up Shakespeare's reference in *King Lear* where the King of France says: 'Not all the Dukes of waterish Burgundy shall take this unprized, precious maid from me.'

But it won't do. Perhaps not many burgundy lovers have allowed themselves to be brainwashed, but the evil influence of the wine investors, who treat fine wine like rare postage stamps, as entries in a ledger of commodities rather than as something which anybody is going to drink, allows the famous producers to put any rubbish into their bottles so long as it has a famous label and an 'approved' year. I would like to think that the bottom is going to fall out of this market when the business expansion schemes start selling their 'investments' in four years' time. At present the only bargains to be found in burgundy are among the parcels of old English-bottled burgundies at auction, and the only worthwhile new burgundies among a tiny band of traditional producers. Remoissenet has never disappointed me, Doudet-Naudin very seldom, and I was delighted to discover among the 1983 tastings that Moillard seems to have seen the light. I wish I could say the same for Clair Daü, Drouhin or even Jadot. But investors are having as bad an effect on burgundy as phylloxera ever did, and until one can convince the world that Romanée-Conti is a wine rather than an investment bond, the future is very bleak.

HOME WINEMAKING IN PIEDMONT

Simon Loftus

Autumn in Piedmont is a marvellous time. The days are bright, the air is crisp and the vintage brings a feeling of satisfying activity. From early morning you come across piles of empty baskets or plastic boxes stacked beside the road, and groups of strong cheerful women, ready to set to work. Later in the day the boxes (filled with grapes) will be lying in the shade of the vines, waiting to be loaded on trucks and trailers, even the occasional ox cart, and taken to the *cantina*. This may be a large co-operative, modern and well equipped, or the modest cellar of an individual grower. It seems that every farm has a barn with a few vats of fermenting must and on the back streets of every village the doors stand open. As you peer from the bright sunshine into the cool darkness of these unsuspected cellars you can smell the fresh grape juice and watch the operations of primitive wine making, essentially unchanged since mediaeval times.

On one such street in the hill village of Roccagrimalda, high above Ovada, the pavement was blocked by a small old-fashioned basket press. Three elderly men were enjoying the sun as they squeezed the last juice out of the red grapes, following the fermentation. Noticing my interest they invited me into the tiny cellar, brought out a bottle of the previous year's wine (with a handwritten label) and insisted that I taste the stuff. The labourer paused in his work at the press and the *padrone* and his friend beamed proudly as I muttered a wholly unmerited compliment on their home-made wine.

It was an entertaining and picturesque scene but it has to be admitted that the end result was almost undrinkable. There was little difference in scale, and none in basic technique, between their wine making and that of the man I had come to see, whose equally simple cellar lay a few doors up the street. Yet their Dolcetto was the worst I have ever tasted, while his is by far the best.

Giuseppe Poggio is a perfectionist with the air of a village grocer. In his stained brown coat he is the sort of man you would expect to find behind the counter of an old-fashioned shop, selling everything from vegetables to horse linament: the kindly old fellow who wraps up your bit of cheese with the smiling and courteous deference of one who knows that you won't find better quality in any of the fancy shops or flashy supermarkets.

But this modest man is, in his local way, quite famous. Anyone in the village will direct you to his house and he carries off the most coveted prizes at the Asti wine fair. He is one of those small growers whose name, for enthusiasts of his region's wines, is far better known than his very limited production.

'My preoccupation is to make a good wine, not a lot of wine.' He points to the end of the little cellar: 'Look at this wall of bottles – all my production is there – it's a nice wall, eh?' He makes no more than 700 cases a year, almost all of it Dolcetto.

This, the 'little sweet', is a grape which appears to originate in Piedmont, one of the three varieties that produce all the notable red wines of this region. Nebbiolo makes the grand Barolo and the slightly less grand Barbaresco, wines that have a rich, autumnal complexity, a hint of tar and the capacity for long life. Barbera tends to be unacceptably astringent to the non-Italian palate. Much prized locally, it is, perhaps, the red equivalent of Bourgogne Aligoté, capable of intermittent fascination but frequently mean. Dolcetto makes the quaffing wine, the Italian beaujolais. It is normally drunk within a year or two of the vintage, when you can relish its delicious immediacy, its mouth-filling flavour of ripe fruit which has a refreshing bitterness at the finish.

In Poggio's hands this grape is transformed to make a wine that has an extraordinary depth of character, a rich almost chocolate density of fruit, great length of flavour and the stamina to last well in bottle. He attributes a great deal of the quality to the situation of his vines on the Trionzo hill. 'The wine there is special, it's something in the ground.' He has two vineyards on this rock, one facing south, the other north-west, a total of three hectares. The combination of grapes from both sides of the hill produces, he believes, a better balanced wine.

There is nothing particularly unusual about the vinification of Poggio's Dolcetto unless you count his perfectionism and the fact that the miniature cement *cuves* in which the wine ferments are painted to resemble wooden *bottes*, the large casks that are the source of so many of Italy's vinous woes. The interesting thing is the maturation, which takes place in an extraordinary collection of small oak casks, too miscellaneous in origin to be dignified with the title *barriques*.

The question of *barrique* versus *botte* is a subject of much dispute in Italy. There is debate as to whether the small French-style cask of about fifty gallons' capacity is better than the big Germanic barrel, sometimes made of chestnut, sometimes oak. There is a considerable argument as to whether the smell and taste of new oak is a desirable ingredient in wine and there is a historical dispute: some growers, Poggio included, argue that prior to this century the Italians always used small casks for maturing the wine and that *bottes* were employed only for fermentation. Above all, there are claims and counter claims as to who, among the present generation of wine makers, was the first to experiment with *barrique* ageing.

Giuseppe Poggio is not one of the fashionable candidates in this contest

Giuseppe Poggio, the perfectionist of Roccagrimalda.

but we may as well record that he bought his first *barrique* (actually a two hundred-litre cask of Solvenian oak) in Yugoslavia, in 1970. He is not a fan of new oak, much preferring the effect of second-hand casks, which he buys all over the place. The most unlikely item in his collection is a Scotch whisky cask, formerly a sherry hogshead, which he found in Genoa. It took him ages to get rid of the smell of whisky. He steamed the cask, rinsed it repeatedly with hot and cold water and finally cured it with wine: Dolcetto, Malvoisie, Moscato and Barbera. It took over three weeks of continuous labour.

Most good wine makers have a few eccentric habits and Giuseppe Poggio is no exception. He thinks things out for himself, adapts the old traditions and delights in astonishing the world with the results. Many well-qualified oenologists would refuse to believe that anything good could come out of such scruffy cellars and I have heard an American taster, furious at Poggio's haphazard indifference to hygienic theory, mutter crossly about 'residual sugar'. But the fact of the matter is that he produces the best Dolcetto in Italy. His normal quality was my idea of perfection until I realised that in exceptional vintages he produces minute quantities of something even more remarkable, his *Riserva Speciale*.

Since I had always thought that Dolcetto was his only love, it came as a slight shock to discover that he also plays around with Barbera. His version is dark in colour, with a slight prickle of gas, and has greater generosity than most specimens of this dour grape. Poggio's secret is to leave the lees of his Dolcetto in the vat and to ferment the Barbera on top. He claims this softens its natural astringency.

Giuseppe likes surprises. On my last visit he greeted me like a conjuror about to produce a wholly unexpected treat. We went upstairs to his house to sample the new vintage of Dolcetto, to munch a few *grissini* and to haggle about prices. There on the table, the focus of all attention, was his little baby.

'I am the only producer in the world of this wine.' Giuseppe Poggio untied the cunningly knotted string that held the cork in place and poured the bottle carefully, so as not to disturb the sediment, into half a dozen mismatched glasses. With the attentive air of a proud father he waited for our reaction.

It was delicious; green-gold in colour, scented of honey and elderflowers, gently effervescent. The mouth-filling flavour of ripe greengages was given life and definition by a fresh acidity and a marvellously invigorating bitterness at the finish. Poggio was delighted at our enthusiasm. A smile and a nod, a little clearing of the throat. As he topped up our glasses it was clear that this bottle-fermented sparkler had not been disgorged, for there was sediment at the bottom of the bottle and the wine was now slightly cloudy. Realising that we liked it, Poggio became voluble with enthusiasm.

He explained its history. Years ago this *spumante* was something of a local speciality, made by most of the local growers. Production gradually died out and even the name of the grape variety was forgotten. Only an obscure nickname survived: *Kari-ja L'osü*, the ass's burden.

That is Piedmontese dialect. The Italian translation, *Carica L'Asino*, is what appears on the hand-drawn, photocopied label that adorns Giuseppe's bottle, together with the words *Vino Raro*.

Rare indeed. Poggio has been making the wine only since 1981 and he is the last producer, working from a few unreliable scraps of the old traditions and using a great deal of his own wine making intuition. He has at least managed to find a few rows of the old vines but they don't yield much. There's just enough juice to fill a small cask, sufficient to make two hundred bottles if all goes well. He sells a few bottles locally but essentially it's homemade wine, for enjoying with his friends.

There are moments when I wish I lived in one of those quiet, sunny streets of Roccogrimalda, perched on its cliff in a remote corner of Piedmont. There is a timeless restfulness about the place and the local food is delicious: some of the best pasta in Italy and, in the winter, the pungent

A small old-fashioned basket press still in use in Piedmont.

magic of the white truffle. There would be the constant delight of being able to drop in on Giuseppe Poggio for a glass of Dolcetto, or Barbera, or of Carica L'Asino, the rarest wine in the world. Then I realise that it would also be necessary, from time to time, to take a glass of wine with his neighbours; and the memory of what *they* produce is sufficiently awful to cause me to rejoice in the bleak reality of a February day in east Suffolk. Wine making, on the whole, is best left to the professionals.

AMERICA COLLECTS

Peter D Meltzer

By now, news of the record-shattering 1787 Jefferson Lafite auctioned at Christie's in December 1985 to Christopher Forbes has been engraved in bidding history. That such a bottle should at last be repatriated to America ought to come as no surprise, given its historical significance, the Forbes's celebrated wine cellar and their passion for presidential memorabilia. Their collection not only includes Lincoln's top hat and Jefferson's desk, but also two rather amusing letters about wine penned by Jefferson himself: one to a lady friend advocating wine drinking as a health aid; another dwelling on the evils of alcohol.

Albeit an extreme example, the Lafite purchase nonetheless illustrates a phenomenon which anyone who has scrutinised the course of fine and rare wine auctions over the past five years or so will have noted: a tell-tale increase in American participation at London wine sales. Much as the British may have originated the notion of laying away large quantities of fine wine for future drinking, Americans have evolved a personalised, individualistic approach to wine collecting which warrants elaboration.

It is worth noting that the two previous record-high wine bids were also established by Americans: an 1822 Lafite acquired at Heublein for $31,000 and a jeroboam of 1870 Mouton Rothschild sold by the Texas Art Gallery for $38,000. They appear to have been bought by food or wine professionals for promotional purposes. The rationale is simple enough; a full page advertisement in the *New York Times* alone runs about $15,000, with television costing considerably more. It is thus far cheaper to make front page news across the nation by writing oneself into the record book.

As for the Forbes's, patriarch Malcolm Sr insists he had no intention of breaking records. In fact, he says he would have been much more comfortable if he had received less publicity and quipped, 'Jefferson could have saved me a lot of money if he had *drunk* the Lafite instead of leaving it behind! If anyone had suggested beforehand that I would have spent over $150,000 for a bottle of wine, I would have been aghast. I'm still one who reads a wine list from right to left! I don't enjoy *drinking* my money, and we

The record shattering 1787 Jefferson Lafite auctioned at Christie's in December 1985 for £105,000, as described in the pre-sale catalogue.

AFTERNOON SESSION

On Thursday 5 December 1985

at 2.30 p.m. precisely

THE 1787 Tн.J. LAFITTE

The Property of Mr. Hardy Rodenstock

Château Lafite—Vintage 1787
Pauillac. Pre-1855 classification. Almost certainly bottled at the château

Original hand-blown amber-green glass bottle with slightly pitted sides, striated neck, kick-in base and sharp pontil mark. Similar in type to the French wine bottle c. 1780 illustrated on page 138 of *Understanding Wine Bottles* by Roger Dumbrell (Antiques Collectors' Club and Christie's) but with the elegant waisted sides more typical of Bordeaux. Height approximately 11½ ins. (29 cm.), diameter of base 3½ ins. (9 cm.). One side of the bottle is covered in heavy and firm cellar dust, the other has been cleaned to reveal 'the original wheel engraved script figures and letters '1787 Lafitte Th.J.'. Original wax seal covered with new protective seal; original cork, long but slightly shrunken with age. Level exceptionally high: ½ inch below cork. Colour appears to be remarkably deep for its age.

have no plans to uncork the 1787. Though with its 200th anniversary looming nigh, we do remain flexible.'

Forbes has his own explanation for the strong American presence at fine wine auctions: 'The English have an advantage which we [Americans] don't share: wine has been a way of life for a great deal longer. Their wine cellars go back a lot further than ours. Some have even been passed on for generations. What's more, England is just a channel away from superb wine and port. So the Englishman doesn't have to reach out for the odd bottle – he either has it, or has the common sense to desist when it is unaffordable.'

In the last two decades, America has experienced not only a dramatic increase in wine consumption, but also in wine production. (While it is not our purpose here to track the evolution of the domestic wine industry, it is common knowledge that American varietals have gained international recognition and acclaim, and have garnered a wide following as a result.) These two developments have contributed to a heightened sense of wine consciousness. More recent events, such as the profound concern with health and fitness, have also fostered a fad for wine. Wine savvy could even be said to be a prerequisite of membership in the Yuppy elite. So, to all intents and purposes, in the United States wine collecting is an acquired rather than an inherited pastime. Possibly out of its very newness, Americans have pursued the avocation with a verve unsurpassed in Europe.

Today the largest private wine collections in the world repose in America. (San Diegan Tawfiq Khoury cellars an astonishing 55,000 bottles, New Orleans' Lloyd Flatt houses 30,000 and Marvin Overton of Fort Worth numbers 10,000.) As *The Wine Spectator*'s Grand Awards programme has demonstrated, there are also hundreds of restaurants across the country boasting copious wine lists with an excess of 250 selections; not mere dressing, but a real response to consumer demand for the fine and rare. So are there dozens of wine shops vaunting a broader selection and larger inventory than can be found in St James's or Paris's Madeleine? Clearly, when Americans decide to pursue an avocation, they do so in a very dedicated fashion.

In fairness, America can trace its wine roots to colonial times. Not only did Jefferson display a fondness for 'O'Brien', 'd'Iquiem' and 'Lafitte' (sic) but apparently he persuaded Washington to stock them as well. For that matter, the first president, like the governor of Delaware and many other dignitaries, even tried to cultivate *vinifera* vinestalks. Though the experiments failed, a tide of imports soon began to flow in the wake. By the early 1800s, for instance, New Orleans had gained a reputation as one of the foremost centres in the country for fine food and wine. Its potential as a major market was recognised by the champagne houses, which often dispatched their titled salesmen with hefty expense accounts in order to ensure a flowing supply of bubbly. 'Champagne Charlie' Heidsieck, whose exploits were immortalised in a music-hall refrain, was probably the best known of them all.

But as the temperance movement gained ground in the late nineteenth century (in part because of the rampant alcoholism on the frontier where taverns outnumbered churches by two to one), even wine consumption began to acquire a stigma. For instance, the celebrated artists, Currier and Ives, felt compelled to revise their rendering of 'Washington Bidding

Good-bye to his Troops', to suit the new morality. In the original engraving, a decanter of madeira was prominently displayed and all the officers held their glasses aloft in a toast. In the later version, all traces of alcohol and madeira-inspired cheer were brushed out!

While wine drinking continued into the early twentieth century (one feature of many 'modern' apartment buildings supplanting New York's fashionable Fifth Avenue mansions was a *bona fide* underground *cave* for each tenant), serious cellars were generally limited to a handful of households like the Whitneys, the Astors and the Duponts. Between two world wars, with Prohibition and the Depression, two generations of Americans were effectively denied the pleasures of wine. While speakeasies may have dispensed a spate of bathtub booze, and clandestine champagne deliveries from St Pierre and Miquelon continued unabated for the duration of Prohibition, period accounts show little call for classic claret or burgundy whatsoever.

Indeed, when wine and spirits shops finally reopened after repeal in 1934, their owners soon discovered that scotch and soda, the Manhattan, and the martini were the alcoholic beverages of preference, even with dinner. Pioneers of the American wine trade like Sam Aaron and Alexis Lichine recall with amusement their efforts in persuading customers even to sample a bottle of wine. Lichine says this country was a wasteland when it came to wine. Aaron remembers his reticence at taking a gamble on 1929 Latour and Mouton for about $1 a bottle! There simply was no consumer interest. Even early Hollywood classics reveal a certain vinous naiveté: In *Made for Each Other*, starring a very youthful Jimmy Stewart and Carol Lombard, Judge Doolittle, 'a noted wine connoisseur' comes to dinner. What does Stewart serve? Why the judge's favorite, a bottle of sparkling red burgundy! Of course.

The years following the Second World War saw more Americans journey abroad than ever before. But it took more than a glass of beaujolais in a Paris café to change the tastes of the American palate. The five-day work week, increased leisure and jet travel all played their part. But in terms of a single event, most contemporaries cite the 1959 vintage in France (hailed at the time as the *vendange* of the century by the French Minister of Agriculture) as a turning point in the evolution of American wine habits. Above all, the harvest received a tremendous amount of press coverage, and bright talk of building a wine cellar soon supplanted gloomy thoughts of other underground facilities such as fallout shelters.

From the outset, American wine enthusiasts went about their collecting with extraordinary intensity and zeal. You might say they were trying to make up for lost time. 'No sooner had I assembled many of the classics I had read about in the works of Harry Waugh and the like than I began to be aware of other chronological gaps and deficiencies and started filling in', says Tawfiq Khoury of his beginnings. Another rationale for the depth and breadth of American wine collectors' cellars (most top American cellars are exceedingly eclectic; not restricted to classic classified growths, but extended to include German, Italian and, of course, native California releases) is an innate tendency to master or dominate any endeavour which happens to captivate their attention or imagination. It's worth noting that there are already a substantial number of young wine collectors under forty who have amassed cellars in the 2,500-4,000 bottle range, despite both inflation and the relative scarcity of classic vintages.

Near St. Bodolph in the
Savoie.

The fourteenth century
château at Gageac near
Bergerac.

Opposite above
Sancerre with the famous
sauvignon blanc vines.

Opposite below
Bergères-lès-Vertus south
of Epernay.

The vineyard of Clos du Pape and the remains of Châteauneuf-du-Pape.

Not only do Americans display a thirst for wine, but they also exhibit a hunger for wine knowledge. There are nearly 500 full-time writers in the United States, and just about every major newspaper now carries a wine column. Monographs, newsletters, monthlies, even bi-weeklies exclusively devoted to wine, count loyal followings in the tens of thousands. Dozens of wine schools can be found both in major centres and small communities. It's no surprise that the dedicated collector can discourse effectively not only on the merits of diverse vintages, but also on the varietal content of a specific release, its Ph factor, volatile acidity, and brix.

Another innovation of the American wine collector has been the 'mega' wine tasting, initiated over a decade ago with Dr Marvin Overton's much touted thirty-vintage vertical examinatioin of Château Latour. Overton ascribes the origins of the event not to Texan largesse, but logical experimentation: 'How could one possibly learn about the plethora of fine vintages by plodding along with flights of six wines at a time?' His Latour extravaganza was followed a few years later by an in-depth vertical of thirty-three Lafites dating back to 1799! Lloyd Flatt has held similar homages to Cheval Blanc and, most recently, Château Pétrus, with a resounding fifty-vintage vertical of Mouton-Rothschild in the works.

Asked why he would deplete his cellar of such treasured prizes, Flatt replied unhesitatingly, 'I mentally expense all my acquisitions at the moment of purchase. What's more, I derive great pleasure out of tasting wines in the company of like-minded friends. It's educational; an opportunity to share and exchange views, and to compare our impressions with what has been recorded.' It's no surprise that Messrs Overton, Flatt and Khoury, in conjunction with other members of 'The Group' (as they call their loosely knit association) have frequently assembled extraordinary rarities at no charge to any participant, for the sole purpose of sampling and enjoying unusual wines. As Michael Broadbent himself has commented, '[These men] answer the oft-repeated question, "What do the purchasers of arcane vintages do with them?" Why they drink them, of course.'

Even wine auctions in America have acquired their own original stamp. Whereas in the UK, all but a few sales are dominated by trade buyers, in those states where wine auctions are allowed, the reverse is true. They usually attract a full house, and have taken on a festive air, sometimes preceded by special tasting lunches or black tie dinners. Another popular twist has been the development of the charity wine auction – easily a dozen major philanthropic events per annum – which have been known to raise upwards of $125,000 in an evening.

Nearly a century ago, Oxford don and avowed oenophile George Saintsbury wrote that anyone with an income of a couple of hundred pounds a year was expected to stock at least a modest wine cellar. But, whereas in the UK and on the Continent, a good wine cellar was always considered a trapping of civilised living (often along with a country house, horses, hounds, etc.) in America, the tradition had no sooner taken hold than it was uprooted. Thus when a new generation rediscovered fine wine, the pursuit fast gained collectable status in its own right – much like collecting Impressionist art, period furniture or silver. If, as some analysts have suggested, the vogue for antiques was an attempt on the part of the collector to prove ancestry he lacked, then a codicil might be added to the theory that the collector of fine and rare wine is seeking ancestry with *taste*. Thankfully, the American exponent is also tasting what he collects.

"*This O.K. with knackwurst?*"

MY DOURO

Pamela Vandyke Price

It is thirty years since I first went to the Douro. Recently and suddenly widowed, I decided that it was a good idea to go where I could study wine in the daytime and then it would not matter if I had to spend my evenings in a hotel with a book (which has never been a hardship for me anyway).

One young friend in the wine trade said, 'I think you'd better meet my father'. This was Wyndham Fletcher, mention of whom gets the immediate response from those who know him, 'The most charming man in the wine trade!' He was then a director of Cockburn in London. A colleague who had grown up in Portugal wrote to her friends Reggie and Avril Cobb and John and Nan Smithes. So I began by introductions to the respected firms Cockburn Smithies and Martinez-Gassiot.

It was only slightly intimidating. I did not then realize that the press had made a rather poor impression on the port trade when they covered the first visit paid to Oporto by Her Majesty the Queen and His Royal Highness, the Duke of Edinburgh. But it was my good fortune to have been brought up in what, in retrospect, seems an old-fashioned way: when Avril Cobb met me at Oporto airport I was wearing gloves and a hat. (Later I was told that my notes of thanks to my numerous hosts had been an agreeable surprise.) It was and, blessedly, still is, stepping back in time to visit the port trade *in situ* and the gentle courtesy, the observance of many British conventions that ease social contacts and enhance hospitality still prevail. It would be superficial and facetious to say that, whereas thirty years ago, the port trade in Oporto and the lodges in Gaia apologised for not having butlers any longer, now they excuse themselves for not always having living-in domestic staff! Times have changed, though. It is no longer remarkable for members of the port trade to speak good, not merely adequate, Portuguese – and Douro Portuguese too, which has a vocabulary of its own, as brides accustoming themselves to marketing have found

The Douro, 'river of gold', near Meão.

(formerly, I suppose, they gave their orders via a housekeeper). Since the revolution in Portugal there is far more friendship as well as respect between Portuguese port establishments and those of the British. The dams up in the Douro have altered the level and flow of that sly, potentially treacherous 'river of gold', there are electricity and indoor sanitation in even isolated *quintas* and I do not think that, these days, women are forbidden the premises 'up country' at vintage time, as Cockburn's certainly did when I first visited them. (Perish the notion – but I've even seen young women treading the grapes these days!)

David Delaforce's grandfather is thought to be the first British port shipper to have married a Portuguese lady: Robin Reid, of Croft, not only married the delectable Elsa, as beautiful as she is accomplished, but he plays jazz drums and tympany at celebrations, to the delight of all. The minute railway which brings visitors up to Pinhão (the roads still wind so that speed is impossible, to the amazement of American tourists, who expect to do the journey in an hour) is greeted by those who water ski alongside the track and there are still discussions about 'trodden' ports and those made by the auto-vinificator. Michael Symington, of Bomfim, relates the trepidation with which he and his brother submitted the first samples coming from this 'newfangled device' to their father, who, after serious appraisal, approved them.

Yet the astonishing, savage country, improbable as the birthplace of a great wine, doesn't change much, in spite of the dams, the overhead cables and the level of the somewhat tamed river. I expected to be impressed. I

still do not know why I think it wonderful. The Douro Valley must be grim in winter, but there's something that calls, appeals, comforts even the least likely persons – such as myself.

An idyllic picnic by the Douro.

Reggie Cobb and John Smithes took me up the Douro, first by train then by car. There was a Portuguese driver – at that time essential for shippers going around the farms, inspecting, buying and preserving a certain quiet dignity. Reggie's niece came with us. Now, I realise, she and I chaperoned each other – it would have been quite improper for a youngish woman or a young girl to have travelled alone with two men; even in Oporto, I discovered, I couldn't go out on my own without attracting a respectful but curious crowd whenever I stopped to look in a shop window. (Avril Cobb told me I should have worn sunglasses, a hat and a big enveloping coat, but even then the escort of a chauffeur or, ideally, another woman or respectable man was advisable).

At the Cockburn *quinta*, at Tua, our rooms were furnished with the washstands and brass-knobbed bedsteads of a century before. Mosquito nets swathed the beds and I still crave for them: more picturesque and, for me with the visitor's blood that lures the whining stinger, more efficacious than sprays and ointments. There was no electricity. If we wished to 'get up in the night', our hosts informed us, we should waken them, so that they could escort us to the bottom of the garden where a 'convenience' – with two seats side by side – was situated. (I was thankful that, for me, the chamberpot in the night table sufficed).

After dinner we sat out in the dark. The insinuating fragrance of the

Douro night is something I can never forget; several visits later, when staying with the Symingtons, I kept on waking because of the wonderful smell of sheets dried out in the open. We swam in the Douro, me in a long-legged woollen bathing dress loaned by the bailiff's wife, everyone else in their underwear. Dozens of pairs of eyes would have seen had we risked going without clothes and, to this day, those who have installed swimming pools deprecate extremes of lack of modesty that may offend the locals who, I think, have a countryfolk's attitude to the conduct congruous with that of 'ladies and gentlemen'.

We were taught to shout where we'd come from – 'Tua! Tua!' – at the dogs who ran barking after our car. At every stop, children brought out the watermelons they knew Reggie loved and I was shown how, if one just ripe is put in the sun, it will become deliciously cool inside. We walked through a railway tunnel to visit one farm, long strides bridging sleepers and a guide, bearing a flaring torch, courteously lending me his arm throughout.

Then, one time when I was exhausted after a long worrying stint of work, Martini & Rossi sent me to stay at Quinta do Noval. For five days in July I was alone there – and I'd forgotten to pack my Portuguese phrase book. The children, both of the estate and the family, when they arrived for the weekend, would leap down from one white-walled terrace to another, but I was so tired that, the first morning, I realised that if I didn't retrace my steps after a short walk, I wouldn't have the strength to get back to the house! One afternoon it was so hot that I had to finish my siesta on the ground floor – 'heat rises'. Each morning the bailiff would drive me down to the reservoir-cum-pool notched into the mountain side and fed by a stream so that, if you were thirsty, you swam under the jet of cool water and opened your mouth. Each evening I'd say goodnight to the little girl who, smiling, had stood behind my chair at dinner and then outside, under the cypress shown on so many pictures of Noval, I'd sip my glass of port and watch the lights coming up in the valley below. Opposite there was a small village, with pink-, white- and one green-walled house, like the cut-out toys of a child's village. The quiet seeped into me. I knew I'd never forget the Douro.

One vintage time I had the luck to be invited to seven different *quintas*. At some I saw the vintage start. The pickers, led by a band of musicians – the accordionist gets paid most because he will, at need, play all night as the treading goes on in the cooler temperature – would dance up to the main house, then disperse to their quarters. Then there were the properties where the vintage was ending – the workers, with garlands, would dance up to the house again, to present their flowers and receive gifts before having a farewell feast.

I came to know the beginnings of new vineyards. When Bruce Guimaraens drove me in a landrover that bucked like a bronco over the as yet unbulldozed earth, I saw why Taylor's headquarters in Pinhão is known as the first-class waiting-room – their windows give on to the station platform, itself muralled with blue and white *azulejos*, the tiles that portray local scenes and ceremonies so enchantingly. At Vargellas I exclaimed at the freshly crisp decor within the traditional house and was shown the difference between trodden port and that coming from the auto-vinificator – would that I had remembered when, in the Hunter Valley in Australia, Murray Tyrrell offered me two glasses and I got them the wrong way round, when trying to appraise mechanically-picked wines against hand-gathered ones!

At Eira Velha, poised above Pinhão, I watched the treading in the unique circular *lagares* framed by blue and white tiles, and sniffed at what is, even after years of neglect, an unmistakable 'English garden' fragrance outside.

Sitting in the garden at Roeda – 'diamond in the necklace of the estates that are the jewels of the Douro' – I heard from Elsa Reid of her Portuguese childhood and, like two Japanese ladies, we watched the gigantic harvest moon float above us. It was Elsa who took me up to the astonishing 'round house' that tops the peak shown in so many pictures of Pinhão, an apotheosis of modernity that is yet bravely in keeping; it was she who arranged for me to visit Carvalhas, across the river from Roeda. Here, is an avenue of almond trees leading to the house and the chapel. This was planted by an ancestor of the present owners when he became betrothed (one cannot, here, use the modern word 'engaged') so that, at her wedding, his bride should drive under and across the shower of pink and white blossoms.

I went to swim at Quinta La Rosa – 'The pool is said to be so deep you can't reach the bottom', said the awed children of the household – and I stayed at the Sandeman house in a tiny village, where, though there was electric light and running water, the furniture was reassuringly similar to that of my grandparents' house. This was modern by comparison with one at Roncão, where the dining-room's mahogany gleamed as if the broadclothed gentlemen from Gaia had only minutes before gone out to see to their ponies for the night, prior to settling around the decanters. Here, the 'kitchen sink' was a stone receptacle that must have changed little for two or three centuries and the bailiff's wife, carrying glasses for our tasting, walked cheerfully behind 'the men' as a matter of routine.

Why hasn't somebody written a book about the Douro wives? Portuguese and British, they deserve a not-so-slim volume. Some, abruptly transported from the UK, have had to adapt to a way of life that is extraordinarily different, and much more time is spent by women in the *quintas* up the Douro these days. Telephones ring – 'Should I pack sweaters?' – from someone coming up to someone installed and braving what can be savage weather. There are few places to stay 'up country' so, as in former times, privileged visitors lodge with friends, handed from one *quinta* to another; hostesses may suddenly have to receive a dozen or more people 'for drinks', or need to extend a dinner for ten to one for sixteen or more, sometimes 'borrowing' staff for big parties. Even in these days of deep freezes, convenience foods and appliances that speed the processes of the kitchen, a *quinta* may still depend largely on its own produce. Cooks and hostesses vie happily with each other in creating superlative country fare, just as hosts and the farmers from whom they buy wine – a mere handshake, instead of any contract, surviving in business done between firms and families for over a century or more – will vie about wines. Sometimes there is a port which has been kept up country and is therefore surprisingly different from anything cellared and blended in Gaia; sometimes there are the fine old tawnies – vintage port is, somehow, never quite as satisfactory a drink in the Douro as in our chillier UK climate – and the women of the establishment, not often banished these days as the port decanters appear, take part in the comments and instruct visitors such as myself in the differences between the various wines in the top quality ranges. There are also, now, discussions about the table wines, the various *consumos*, of the Douro, which have always been house drinks but which are now proving as popular in export markets as they were when our ancestors discovered them to be warming to the marrow of their bones.

Wine is a commodity of hope – the next vintage, the next vineyard, the next 'little improvement' in the winery. So I hope to see other *quintas*, the Portuguese establishments: Ferreira (dominated by the traditions of the great lady of port, Doña Antonia), Calém, Ramos Pinto, Rozès and many more. Once again I want to walk over those vineyards of granite schist and smell, among the other Douro flowers, the aromatic gum cystus. When, in 1978, Croft celebrated their tercentenary, the wives of all the port shippers garlanded the great staircase in the Oporto Factory House with the wild flowers of the Douro – they must have competed strongly with the bouquet of any wines served on that historic evening.

How much I should like to go on another boat trip up the river, passing Tua and, in the greenish evening light, drift down to Pinhão and a leisurely dinner. I want to wander in the odd mediaeval town of São João da Pesquiera (St John the Fisherman) and buy the produce of the superlative pork butcher there or, from any Douro bakery, a loaf of bread; for Portuguese bread is the champion loaf among most of the vineyard regions I've visited, rivalled only, maybe, by the wholemeal bakings of the estates in the Cape vineyards of South Africa.

Of course, I also want to see the new vineyards, to know whether the up-and-down strip type of cultivation, influenced by Lenz Moser, is as successful as the expensive terracing; I want to sample the wines made from ungrafted vinestocks which, tufty and seemingly dilapidated when viewed from afar, may, in these days of clonal selection, achieve the soft, profound style of pre-phylloxera ports. The kiddie-car sized tractors wander cautiously along the terraces that are still, somehow, maintained – and how I should like to have a dress made from a photoprinted fabric of an aerial view of one of these contoured vineyards!

Back in someone's *quinta*, there will be *caldo verde*, 'lawn mower soup', that odd, soothing cabbage recipe, individual to whoever makes it, and, after dinner, I would like to go outside where I can feel that the stars are only a long arm's reach away, while I sip my port. The tipped-back wooden armchairs in which we will sit have wide arms to hold glasses, or even decanters and, I suppose, they have been made to a pattern from the more upholstered period and the plumpness of our ancestors throughout what is now as dated as the 'British Raj'.

In the bookcases on the landings and on the bedside shelves there will be pre-1914 numbers of long-dead periodicals and first editions of nineteenth-century novels will prop up the sagging paperbacks of the present day, bestowed by more recent travellers.

How can I – why do I – love the Douro so much?

Even without the presence of dear friends, there is something wonderful about the summer landscape. During the Second World War, shippers told me, as, I suppose, their grandfathers might have said or, even, their great-great-grandfathers, might have (in the somewhat incoherent ever-so-British jerked-out syllables) tried to say: there is something here as indefinable as love. Those of us fortunate enough to have known it, even for days, long to go back.

Reggie Cobb saw electric light put in at Tua where, recently, Nan and

John Smithes entertained me – maybe John hasn't the champion length of spit of the port trade these days, but the gentleness, the sensitivity to the wines being made is still the same. At Cockburn's modern Quinta da Santa Maria, Reggie was always welcome. When the firm decided to 'declare' the 1983 port vintage, they brought Reggie a glass of the young, purple-black wine to sniff and sample. He'd been blind for some years and it was only a few weeks before, years after Avril's death, he died too. Those who were there told me that Reggie inhaled, raised his glass and smiled at those whom he could no longer see.

Oporto from the terrace of the Delaforce lodge.

'I say – *that*'s the Douro!'

A great fragrance and a great wine are heartening to take into the dark.

AUSTRALIA – QUALITY AND VERSATILITY

James Halliday

Thirty years ago one or two enlightened Australian *vignerons* and wine makers embarked on a voyage of discovery. They sailed seemingly uncharted seas, their deeds neither understood nor appreciated by the majority of their contemporaries. But they persevered, and within a decade had been joined by a growing number of argonauts. The voyage of discovery, too, turned out to be in part a voyage of rediscovery of lost civilisations.

The once-proud districts of the high Adelaide Hills in South Australia, almost all of central and southern Victoria (including the Yarra Valley, Geelong, Bendigo, the Pyrenees, East Gippsland, the Mornington Peninsula) and Tasmania were devoid of vineyards in 1955. Yet they had been significant, if not famous, wine regions in 1885. Likewise, the noble grape varieties of *chardonnay, pinot noir* and *cabernet-sauvignon* had been grown 100 years ago, only to disappear in the oenological dark age which gripped this country for the first half of the twentieth century.

Now, in 1985, cool climate areas are flourishing once again, and those noble varieties (assisted by *sémillon, sauvignon-blanc, shiraz* and the other members of the *cabernet* family) provide virtually all of the quality base-material for our wines. So it is that Australian wine of 1985 can be argued to have more in common with that of 1885 than 1955.

Fine table wine has replaced ferruginous and somewhat smelly 'burgundies' – a euphemism, if ever there was one – and a veritable lake of fortified wine. (It is a little-known but remarkable fact that between 1928 and 1938 the United Kingdom imported more wine from Australia than it did from France. Almost all of this Australian wine was fortified.)

In one sense, the real innovations of the past thirty years have been technical. During this time Australian wine makers and academics have gained a world-wide reputation among their peers (even if not among

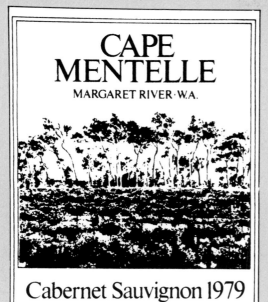

CAPE MENTELLE

MARGARET RIVER · W.A.

Cabernet Sauvignon 1979

PRODUCED AND BOTTLED BY
CAPE MENTELLE VINEYARDS PTY. LTD. MARGARET RIVER
WESTERN AUSTRALIA

E. & P. Pratten

1980
Capel Vale
cabernet
sauvignon

WINEMAKERS COMMENTS:
An elegant, balanced light bodied dry red wine with the varietal fruit character of Cabernet Sauvignon grapes grown at Capel Vale vineyard on the S.W. Coast.
Produced at Capel Western Australia by E & P. PRATTEN – HJ82

CAPEL VALE WINES
P.O. BOX 692 BUNBURY 6230

750 ml

PETALUMA

1980 COONAWARRA

745ml

PRODUCE OF AUSTRALIA BOTTLED AT PICCADILLY SA

TIM KNAPPSTEIN'S ENTERPRISE WINES

CLARE VALLEY
CABERNET SHIRAZ
1980 VINTAGE

1980
CABERNET SHIRAZ

A blend of 70% Cabernet Sauvignon and 30% Shiraz, this wine is made entirely from grapes grown on the Enterprise vineyards 3 km south-east of Clare. Bottled in February 1982 after 11 months ageing in American oak puncheons it is a big rich flavoured wine, full bodied and yet well balanced with acid and tannin. We predict a long life for this wine and recommend cellaring for at least five years to help reach its full potential.

Silver Medal   Class 22   Canberra 1981
Bronze Medal   Class 7   Brisbane 1980

WINEMAKER

1980
Balgownie

Hermitage

GROWN, MADE AND BOTTLED AT BALGOWNIE VINEYARD
BENDIGO, VICTORIA

Proprietors: S. Anderson & Son

ALCOHOL 11.8° BY VOL.   750 ml.

Vineyards at Yeriberg in the
Yarra Valley near
Melbourne.

Opposite
The old winery of Chateau
Tahbilk is believed to have
been built in 1887.

consumers at large) for the excellence of their wine-making techniques and
their wine research. Yet even here, the most important change in red wine
making – the deliberate introduction of new oak flavour in red wine
through the use of new *barriques* and hogsheads for maturation – was no
more than a conscious duplication of French techniques. It is now so much
an integral part of standard wine making practice there is a danger that the
debt due to its Australian pioneer, Max Schubert, will be forgotten.

Moreover, Schubert also preached the gospel of fruit flavour, magically
replacing rather tired, roasted and brown-coloured wines held together by
awesome quantities of alcohol and tannin, with red-purple wine redolent of
berries, rich in texture and high in fruit, oak and tannin flavours. Schubert's
creation of Penfolds Grange Hermitage, which then and now encapsulates
all these characteristics, is nonetheless now seen by some to be a somewhat
extreme approach to style. While undeniably a great wine, current
wine-making wisdom favours a slightly less forthright approach, seeking to
retain fruit flavours but also to introduce elegance.

The first Grange Hermitage was made in 1952; the following year saw the
introduction of the first pressure white-wine fermenter in Orlando's
Rowland Flat Winery, laying the seeds for a transformation in white-wine
style and quality no less radical than that of red wine. In the ensuing thirty
years oxidation has been all but banished from Australian wineries, and
fruit flavour scrupulously protected.

Nineteen-fifty-three also witnessed the rebirth of Coonawarra; in that

The observation tower and winery of Michelton in the Goulburn valley, Victoria.

year Ronald Haselgrove visited Bill Redman for the first time and purchased red wine for Mildara. Two years later he returned to purchase land, predicting – with great prescience – that within a few years every major wine company in Australia would be clamouring for a piece of its terra rossa soil. History shows that Coonawarra (and its next door neighbour, Padthaway) are now Australia's most important quality wine regions.

So three of the strands were woven within a year or two of each other. The fourth came ten years later, when Dr Max Lake planted *cabernet-sauvignon* on the bright red soil of Lake's Folly in the Hunter Valley and became the first of (literally) hundreds of weekend *vignerons*. Fourth strand it may be, but it certainly heralded a remarkable polarisation in the Australian wine industry between the very big companies on the one hand and the small-to-medium concerns on the other. In my *Australian Wine Compendium* (published 1985) there are 430 winery entries: sixty-five of these wineries produce ninety-eight per cent of all Australian wine, leaving two per cent from the remaining 365 producers.

At this point debate intensifies, with the big companies showing distinct signs of irritation at the press (and consumer) attention given to the small producers. A recent market survey showed that only six per cent of wine consumers thought the large companies produced the best wines, a distinctly jaundiced view, and not supported by the facts. Take

Chardonnay, for example: national wine-show results and major newspaper and magazine tastings consistently place Lindemans Padthaway Chardonnay, Orlando RF Chardonnay and Seppelts Chardonnay (all three being very large companies) in the top half dozen Chardonnays in the country, leaving hundreds of other more highly priced Chardonnays floundering in their wake.

Why, then, do the wines of the big companies have such an indifferent reputation? The answer is simple. In a country in which seventy-five per cent of all wine is sold in a 'cask' or flagon, wine has been treated as just another supermarket beverage, distinguished from coca-cola, beer and toilet rolls only by the irrational and savage discount wars which have succeeded in reducing the price of wine per millilitre to less than that of coke or beer. Those casks and flagons are made and marketed by the big companies, whose baked-bean-mentality sales managers are quite unable to perceive that a quality bottled wine should be treated any differently. So it is that midway through 1985 the exemplary 1984 Orlando RF Chardonnay sold at retail for as little as $3 a bottle, and Orlando's current advertising campaign understandably suggests that if you buy anything else, you are paying too much.

The serpent in this consumerist Garden of Eden is that the wine companies, both large and small, have been making a grossly inadequate return on funds. There are inexorable pressures on costs which have the most serious implications for quality in the medium-to-long-term if current trends are not speedily reversed. The final irony is that the wine industry has achieved all this despite an increase in per capita consumption of table wine from two to twenty litres in the past two decades, and – even more importantly – without any signficant competition from imports. Exports and imports are roughly equal, at around five per cent of total production. (We have a strong streak of the Irish in our national ancestry.)

There is a silver lining to most clouds, I guess. Both the demise of the Australian dollar at the end of 1985, and the depressed prices on the local market, must encourage Australian wine makers to take a far more positive attitude to exports. In consequence, the quality of the best Australian wines should become far better known overseas.

But not all wines will find ready acceptance in world markets. Rhine Riesling, for example, remains the backbone of Australian white-wine production once one moves out of casks and into bottled wine. Nonetheless, in its traditional mould, made dry and with a steely strength which can provide surprisingly longevity, this very Australian wine does not fit into any conventional pattern and is not generally understood – or appreciated – outside this country.

The advent of *botrytis*, now a yearly occurrence in Coonawarra and Padthaway, may provide a partial salvation. We are producing a scintillating array of wines of beerenauslese weight, which are prophets without honour in Australia. There is no better example of this than the de Bortoli sauternes (made from "botrytised" *sémillon* grown at Griffith, in the very hot Murrumbidgee Irrigation Area), which is now sold principally in the United States at prices which could never be obtained on the domestic market. Names to watch in the "botrytised" Riesling style are Yalumba Heggies, St Huberts, Thomas Hardy Collection Series, Petaluma and Seppelts (the last two from Padthaway).

Hunter Valley Sémillon never ceases to amaze visitors from overseas,

The Rothbury Estate in the Hunter Valley, New South Wales, with its impressive modern winery.

particularly when they taste a fifteen-year-old example made by Lindemans. In more recent years, Rothbury Estate has carried the flame, with its '72, '73 and '79 vintages quite outstanding. Tyrrell, Saxonvale and Rosemount add to the range of subtly differing styles, all making contributions of merit. They are all wines which will travel well.

In 1971 Tyrrell made and marketed the first Chardonnay for 100 years or so, establishing his famed Vat 47 Pinot Chardonnay (sic). Now, fourteen years later, *chardonnay* is grown in every Australian wine region and obligingly produces a wine of merit in every one. The style varies considerably from the fine and elegant wines of cool climates such as Tasmania and the Yarra Valley (with Lilydale Vineyards an outstanding producer) through to the peaches-and-cream wines of McLaren Vale and the Hunter Valley. In the lower Hunter, Murray Tyrrell rules the roost (with small wineries such as Peterson and Brokenwood adding a dimension), while Rosemount dominates proceedings in the Upper Hunter.

But whether it be Padthaway in South Australia, Margaret River (and Leeuwin Estate), Capel Vale or Moss Wood in Western Australia or any of the other forty or so wine regions, *chardonnay* thrives. In weight the wines are closer to those of California than to those of France, with oak looming large on the flavour horizon – perhaps a little too large for those not familiar with the style. The wines also incline to be somewhat precocious, blooming early but tending to fade after three or four years in bottle. There are still challenges to be met, notwithstanding the great successes of Australian Chardonnays in comparative tastings held around the world in the past year or two.

Sauvignon Blanc, usually blessed by oak in best Mondavi tradition, is the market darling of the moment. For American palates we do fairly well with the wine; for those who accept Sancerre as a benchmark, New Zealand has a mortgage on the variety.

Pinot Noir is as elusive a quarry as it is everywhere outside (and even

The old still in the open-air museum at Bailey's Winery, Bundarra, Victoria.

inside) Burgundy. The Yarra Valley has given the best results so far (with Yarra Yering Vineyard in the vanguard in 1982 and 1983, and Yarra Burn Vineyard in 1984), although Stuart Anderson of Balgownie at Bendigo in Victoria (in 1980 and 1984) and Dr Bill Pannell at Moss Wood in the Margaret River (in 1981) made outstanding wines. Andrew Pirie at Pipers Brook and Julian Alcorso at Moorilla Estate seem intent on proving that Tasmania can do even more with the variety than the Yarra Valley. But these are the only bright spots in a sea of otherwise unrelieved gloom.

Cabernet Sauvignon is the great traveller of the wine world, its regal and masculine personality asserting itself wherever it goes. Many fine Cabernets are made across Australia every year, less tannic and more supple than their Californian counterparts, and worthy of comparison with all but the greatest wines of Bordeaux. It seems unfair to single out names, but Petaluma, Enterprise, Cullens, Cape Mentelle, Hollick, Balgownie and Mount Mary are small winery names which are famous in Australia, although little known outside. The Bordeaux blend-mates of *merlot* and *cabernet franc* have only been sparingly propagated to date, but both the demands of the market-place (and the ambitions of wine makers) will see these produced in greater quantities over the remainder of this decade.

Shiraz – or Hermitage, as it is often called here – has fallen from public esteem. As visitors from England and America are often quick to point out, this is thoroughly undeserved. There are three distinct styles of Shiraz: the smooth, velvety and often slightly smelly wines of the Hunter Valley and other warm regions, traditionally labelled burgundy and – at least in terms of structure – going close to justifying the use of that term. Then there are the rich and chewy wines headed by Grange Hermitage. Thirdly, and most recently, there are the fragrant crushed pepper/spice versions, usually emanating from the 'cool corner' of Australia, and emulating those great reds from the top end of the Rhône Valley.

Finally, just to prove that we wine makers in Australia can do everything, the country produces superb sherries (ranging from fino to amoroso), ranking only after those of Jerez; tawny and vintage ports second only to those of the Douro; and fortified muscats and tokays which yield pride of place to no country. The problem is to persuade enough people around the world to savour the delights of such wines; not surprisingly, Australia has had by far the greatest success with those gloriously rich and raisined muscats and tokays.

Australia supports a very large population of kangaroos without effort; has larger snow fields than Switzerland; sails twelve-metre yachts with a degree of success; and (in the eyes of some, most paradoxically of all) makes great wine.

CORSICA –
ILE DE BEAUTÉ

Hugh Johnson

The French have shown their fastest turn of speed, that inimitable blend of romanticism and salesmanship, in thinking up names for their new *vins de pays.*

Who can resist a wine from the Jardin de la France or the Valleé du Paradis (respectively the Loire valley and the southern Corbières), let alone the uniquely evocative Ile de Beauté? Can you not picture the sirens on the shore – and I do not mean nudists from Kaiserslautern? They have caught it in a phrase, the magic mystic island. It scarcely matters where these wines come from, or even if the island is a figment of the imagination.

But l'Ile de Beauté is real, and really beautiful. Its name is Corsica. Parts are so dramatic and savage that they rival the Alps. The summit of the island, Monte Cinto, rears its bare back, seldom free of snow, to over 8,000 feet, within only fifteen miles of the coast. The streams tearing down from the mountainous backbone of the island have cut deep gorges whose naked rock supports astonishing trees. Europe's biggest, tallest and oldest pines grow here in places where a harebell or a tuft of grass would find it hard to lodge. The black pine of Corsica grows straight as a spear wherever it germinates, whether in pillared groves on deep soil or as an impossible-looking exclamation mark halfway up a thousand-foot cliff.

On the softer, lower slopes, sweet chestnut trees spread their limbs over half an acre at a time, shading with their pale green, in autumn straw and squirrel brown, the rootings of a race of hairy porkers as lean as labradors. A diet of chestnuts and the exertions of mountain life make their ham flavoury and lean – and wonderful exercise for the jaw.

On my first visit to the island, twelve years or so ago, I was vastly smitten by its beauty, but expected little of its wines, and found less. It was November, and I was sussing it out for a visit the following spring by the *Sunday Times* Wine Club in force, the biggest force the club has ever sent on

The Gulf of Porto with the rose-coloured mountains dropping sheer to the deep blue sea.

a single sortie, in fact: a halycon Mediterranean cruise that still lingers in the memories of us old-timers.

On my third visit, last summer, I was all agog to see the forests again, and ready to make use of some of the Mediterranean's cleanest and most attractive beaches – but my interest had been aroused by passing references I had heard in Paris to wines of unique and excellent character. I was told categorically that France's best sweet muscat was made on Cap Corse at the northern tip of the island. Stranger, that the same bleak promontory produces dry whites of high quality. Not so strange, perhaps, that the red and robust rosé of the island's traditional hillside vineyards (as opposed to its new mass-production ones on the flat east coast) were beginning to show real character and form. France's past wine literature, as far as I can discover, has steadfastly ignored Corsican wine. Now it seems things are changing. So I took the ferry from Nice to Ajaccio with pleasant anticipation, if not exactly high hopes.

I fell into the right hands straight away – those of the Comte de Poix, inheritor of an eighteenth-century 'palace' on the Ajaccio seafront and a *domaine* in the hills overlooking the capital's splendid curving bay. I say inheritor because the Domaine Peraldi belonged to his grandmother. His professional life was spent as an industrious (and industrial) Parisian, married to the daughter of a famous Champagne house. Here he was for the summer, past retirement age but working seven days a week in broiling heat. Not, you can be sure, just to add to France's lake of nondescript reds and rosés.

If Louis de Poix is driven, it is by the knowledge of marvellous potential. When he arrived he tasted the wines of his scattered wine-growing neighbours around Ajaccio, south at Sartène, right up north at Patrimonio – and realised that Corsia's own grapes, on Corsica's best vineyard soil, have flavours as fine and resonant as any of the classics of the Mediterranean. At Ajaccio and on the west coast it is principally the *sciacarello*; at Patrimonio principally the *nielluccio*, apparently the form of the *sangiovese* of Tuscany (another of whose close relations is the *brunello* of Montalcino). The custom has been to blend their juice with enough of the lucky-dip of Midi varieties, *carignan grenache, cinsaut* and the rest, to neutralise pretty well the character of the local grape. Increase the proportion, though, and a wine emerges that will one day put Corsica on the serious wine map.

Hints of a better past are there if you like to look for them. The little rattling railway that links Ajaccio and Bastia across the forested ridges climbs steadily out of the capital to what was once the summer resort of the *haut-bourgeoisie* – at three thousand feet among the pines a cluster of villas around the station and chapel of Vizzavona. *Vins de garde* were regularly taken up to Vizzavona, even before the railway made it easy, to benefit from the cooler conditions of its rock-cut cellars. History records no direct

Patrimonio takes the prize for scenery, even by Corsican standards.

link between this fact and the surrender of the celebrated bandit, Antoine Bellacoscia, aged seventy-five years, on the platform of Vizzavona station after forty-four years as an outlaw. (He lived on another twenty years in retirement, revered by all, in the chestnut-shaded village of Boscognano, just down the line.)

Louis de Poix might be called the prophet of *sciacarello*. The rosé of his Domaine Peraldi is aromatic with it, and his experimental red, Sciacarello Pur, is stiff and velvety with it. Its flavour is hard to describe; dry yet soft, almost dusty at first sip, then expanding into a peach-and-almond complexity. More extraordinary perhaps even than the flavour of Sciacarello is its effect on the system (yours and mine, that is) – or rather its lack of effect. De Poix mentioned, rather as optimistic old French handbooks do, that the wine was 'easy to digest'. Not many wines give me the colly-wobbles, so at first I thought little of it. Then I realised that I was drinking the best part of a bottle of twelve-degree rosé at lunch, under a hot sun, and feeling cheerier than ever. Imagine what a bottle of Tavel would do: the lapse into listlessness, the short nap, the waking with a splitting head. I found this softly fruity rosé very much to my liking, both on the positive and the negative sides.

An evening tasting of neighbour's wines at a miraculously green little property in the hills (drought and vandal-started fires were a horror story in Corsica last summer) had me convinced that the Peraldi wines are not alone. We tasted, before a feast for which many a porker must have died, a range of reds, rosés and even a white wine as much as eight years old. The oldest Sciacarello, at ten years, was a pale wine of many subtle facets. The white, a Vermentino, was in that rare state of soft nutty richness combined with spring-like freshness that few wine makers of the south have ever managed, and none since cold fermentation came into fashion. When they *have*, they have made something more toothsome than ever came out of a stainless steel vat.

There was enough encouragement here to send me scurrying round the island. In the short time I had between forests (those of Aitone, of Valdoniello, of la Restonica and la Castagnaccia are all required viewing), I managed to visit several more growers on the east coast, make a pilgrimage to Patrimonio in the north, and at least taste, if not visit, the remotest of the island's wines: those at the extreme northern end of Cap Corse.

Patrimonio takes the prize for scenery. Even by Corsican standards the situation of this ancient vineyard is spectacular. Seen from 1,500 feet above, coming down the pass over the mountains from Bastia, with the sun westering, it is a biblical chaos of abrupt sugar-loaf mountains grey and purple in the haze.

Suddenly in their midst, on a minor mound, rises an immensely tall and narrow church, the bare hillsides give way to patches of vines and vegetables and little farmhouses offer *dégustation, vente directe, vins, miel, legumes*. One singular hill dominates the valley where the village lies, planted on the east slope with a vineyard the shape of a grand piano. This prime position, I was told, belongs to Dominique Gentile. I soon tasted his wines: deep Nielluccio red, pale Vermentino white, intense golden muscat. The bad news was that they were sold out. So, apart from the odd bottle, were several other growers we tried. Patrimonio is for the patient, it seems. I shall persist.

It was in the port of Bastia, under huge creamy rectangular parasols at

Opposite
The Old Port at Bastia.

The Col de Vergio
(4,800 feet) and
the Fôret d'Aïtone.

Chez Assunta, that we tasted the white wines of Cap Corse. Clos Nicrosi
and Domaine de Givelli, both at Rogliano, use the *malvoisie*, alias *malvasia* or
malmsey, ancient source of wines of high quality varying from soft and dry
to very sweet, all round the Mediterranean. Cap Corse makes them dry,
very pale, taut with concentrated flavour yet just acidic enough to be
refreshing. They are old-fashioned wines in concentration, coming from
stony vineyards with tiny crops, but modern in their cleanness,
unoxidised, bright in the mouth and well able to mature and grow
succulent in bottle. Needless to say they are gold dust: not another bottle to
be had. Why am I telling you this, then? Because the world of wine is wider
– much wider – and much more wonderful than any of us has yet grasped.
The latest Chardonnay is all very well, but the thrill of a new/old flavour is
worth far more – even with the frustration of having to wait years for an
allocation.

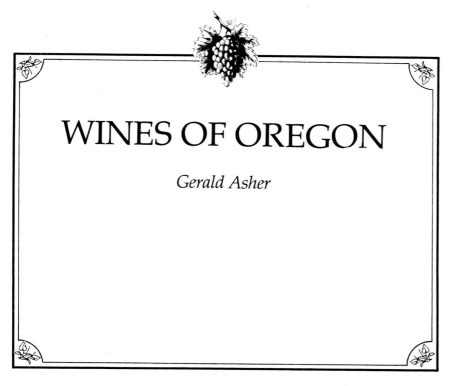

WINES OF OREGON

Gerald Asher

'You'll be frosted out every spring, rained out every fall, and get athlete's foot up to your knees', Maynard Amerine, Professor of Oenology at the University of California, Davis, told David Lett back in 1964, when the young viticulture graduate announced his intention of growing *pinot noir* in Oregon's Willamette Valley. At that time success with *pinot noir* had eluded everyone everywhere else in North America, and, though Richard Sommer, another Davis viticulture graduate, had planted vines near Roseburg in a milder part of the state three years before, there were no vines at all in the Willamette Valley. Lett was undeterred, and, though both he and his vines have had to struggle, in just twenty years he has seen spring from the shoots he planted a major new wine region, where 1,500 acres of vineyards now support twenty-four flourishing wineries. And, as well as the kind of local recognition normally denied prophets, he and those who followed him have gained international respect and honours.

In 1979, in a comparative tasting in Paris, the success of David Lett's Eyrie Vineyard Pinot Noir was confirmed when Robert Drouhin insisted on a re-run on his home ground in Beaune in 1980. Then in the autumn of 1985, a group of New York merchants and writers, tasting blind seventeen assorted Oregon Pinot Noirs and Côte d'Or burgundies, all of the 1983 vintage, gave their preference to three of the Oregon wines ahead of any from the Côte d'Or (which included wines from the Drouhin cellars and from the Comte de Vogüé, among others; no one could say the dice were loaded). And though it has always been possible to question the significance of cross-tasting Bordeaux and California Cabernet Sauvignons because the generally broader structure and more forward style of California tends to put Bordeaux at a disadvantage in such encounters, this is not an argument that can be used to detract from this public acceptance of Oregon's Pinot Noirs. *Pinot noir* grown in Oregon, in fact, has more in

common with its counterpart grown on the Côte d'Or – for better or worse – than Napa Cabernet Sauvignon has with its Médoc sibling. The tasters in New York had difficulty even distinguishing the Oregon Pinot Noirs from the Côte d'Or burgundies, demonstrating at very least a lack both of obvious stylistic differences, and quality levels within reach of each other.

Starting barely half an hour's drive from Portland, the vineyards of Oregon's Willamette Valley nestle among stands of cedar, fir, and alder. In summer the overgrown roadsides are thick with flowering bramble and blue bachelor's buttons, purple vetch, and orange poppies. Clumps of wild lupine and walnut trees line dirt driveways to worn frame houses comfortably settled among rose bushes and cherry orchards; scrawled notices offer milk-goats for sale; and sheep graze and cows ruminate on lush grass that would have had Thomas Hardy fooled. Only the distant peaks of the Cascade Range and an occasional log cabin remind us that this is Little Mary Sunshine country, an Arcadia in the West.

Between the Cascade Range and the Coast range, the Willamette Valley is protected from continental and oceanic excesses while benefiting from the influences of both. Though snow here rarely stays on the ground for more than a few days, winter is easily cold enough for the vines to go dormant. Also, because summer days are tempered by marine air and interspersed with cooling showers, the grapes form slowly, begin to change colour when picking is already under way in California, and ripen only as the long growing season is ending and leaves are ready to fall. Whereas *pinot noir* in California, for example, is, by early September brought swiftly to the degree of sugar-richness at which it must be harvested, it is not ready for picking in the Willamette until October, having been coaxed through later, cooler days to a balance and flavour attainable in no other way. Unhurried maturing through mild autumn weather gives these grapes the intense, crisp flavour that earned for the Willamette its well-established reputation for farm fruits and berries. Like any other fruit farmer, the Willamette wine grower has learned to fret less about sugar levels than about the degree of flavour in his grapes.

If it was the cool Willamette climate that had first attracted David Lett and others, there was also, perhaps, for some of them, a vision of Oregon as a New Jerusalem in which they would save themselves from a California Babylon. But then pioneering is heady stuff, and, if the state code of wine regulations, drawn up and finally agreed on by the growers themselves in 1977, was imbued with more than a whiff of self-righteousness, it also made clear the direction growers intended to follow. Seen, then, as their viticultural manifesto, its fervour is understandable and excusable, despite the tilting at windmills. (European generic names in current coinage, even synonyms like Johannisberg Riesling, are forbidden in Oregon; much was made of the tangle of *gamays*, with or without a hyphenated 'Beaujolais', and of *Pineau de la Loire*, a French name for *chenin* that I have yet to see used in the United States anyway.)

At their core the regulations attempt bravely to establish objectives rather than crystallise experience, as though the authors had forgotten, if they had ever known, how the older appellation systems – also intended to protect unique styles and standards – had come into being. For example, the Oregon regulation concerning Cabernet Sauvignon lays down not only that a wine so labelled must contain seventy-five per cent *cabernet-sauvignon* grapes (an arbitrary limitation because no one has ever shown that a wine

Opposite
The spectacular Multnomel Falls in Oregon.

grown in Oregon is better for having seventy-five per cent rather than, say, sixty-five per cent or even eighty-five per cent *cabernet-sauvignon*) but also that the balancing twenty-five per cent *must* be exclusively *malbec, merlot* or *petit verdot*, the three grape varieties permitted to be used in conjunction with *cabernet sauvignon* in the Médoc. Defiance of California did not, apparently, extend to Bordeaux. How could those who imposed this constraint be so certain that *syrah* grapes, for instance, might not do more than *malbec* for Cabernet Sauvignon in the growing conditions of Oregon? Why did they include *petit verdot*, a variety of minor importance disappearing in France and as yet commercially non-existent in Oregon, and *merlot*, a variety that seems unable to set fruit in the damp Oregon climate? When they have so much to learn about their own potential, why did they put themselves prematurely in a viticultural straitjacket?

A more positive and sharper picture of the pragmatism, perseverance and co-operative achievement of Oregon growers emerges, however, from the projects to which they have since applied themselves. Their superb *Growers' Guide*, for example, as plainly written and illustrated as it is detailed and all-encompassing, passes on to newcomers (and to each other) a compendium of growers' and researchers' practical findings over the past twenty years in Oregon, along with the essentials of what has been learned in other cool-climate growing regions. It is refreshingly free of dogma and gives valuable tips with a disarming encouragement that lends more than mere illumination to the theoretical explanations and drawings. ('Training young vines', begins the author of one section, 'is chronic work; in my mind it is very much like doing the dishes. The work is not terribly difficult, but no matter how much you do, there is always more.')

Together the growers have successfully lobbied through the state legislature a levy on all wine sold and crushed in Oregon, which will fund research specific to the state's viticultural needs and provide a purse from which promotional programmes can be financed. They have produced guide booklets and maps, organised group tasting tours, paid for market research, and sallied forth in a band to New York and elsewhere from time to time in search of distant customers. In the summer of 1984 they persuaded the University of Oregon to sponsor and underwrite an international symposium on Cool Climate Winegrape Growing that drew to Eugene an astonishing number of the world's top academicians and professionals in this field.

The presentations and panel discussions at that symposium were pointed and provoked lively participation from growers who have had to learn from their own trials. When Richard and Nancy Ponzi planted their Beaverton Vineyard in 1970, as they recall, there was little common experience to draw on. 'Some of the other early growers were Davis graduates', Ponzi explained, 'but they had soon found that techniques learned in California had to be adapted to Oregon conditions. We were forever in seminars teaching each other. We learned, for instance, the importance of training our vines vertically to make the most of leaf exposure to light, as opposed to California, where leaves also provide shade both to plant and to fruit. Growers here would like to train their vines even higher – we talk constantly of different kinds of trellises – and to plant more densely so that fewer bunches on each vine would give us the same yield with greater leaf surface for each bunch. It's the leaves that do the vine's work, after all.'

The glacier capped peaks of the towering mountain range form a backdrop for the Western Oregon wine region.

To achieve that density some growers have indeed started a programme of interplanting, using the simple process of layering shoots in the ground to create vines between existing ones (a process possible in phylloxera-free Oregon, where almost all vines grow directly on their own roots without need for grafting onto resistant stock.) David Adelsheim, of Adelsheim Vineyard, has produced comprehensive schedules to demonstrate the ideal narrower row spacing for each variety, which, in conjunction with other factors, will provide optimum quality crop levels. But most growers feel unable to abandon their present ten-foot rows spaced to accommodate American gauge tractors. 'Narrow gauge European tractors are available', said Bill Blosser, of Sokol Blosser Winery, 'but I like to be able to run down for a spare part when I need one and be back on the job in twenty minutes. Parts for European tractors are not easy to find and must usually be flown in.' Adelsheim, who spent some time at the *Lycée Viticole* in Beaune and who led the writing of the state wine regulations, would still like to see narrower rows. 'In setting up we made some early mistakes', he says quite simply.

Mistakes or not, most of the Oregon wines I have tasted have been good to outstanding, with few disappointments – though that proportion could change, I suppose, had I the opportunity to drink them more often. A recent article in *The Oregonian*, in fact, quotes one or two out-of-state wine writers who criticise the state's wines for lack of consistency and failure to live up to glowing reports. 'Part of the problem', wrote Matt Kramer, 'lies with the fact that only a handful of the state's best wines escape the orbit of the local market … [And] too often the praise for Oregon wine can exceed (or at least distort) what we sometimes find in the bottle.' But it is always the few outstanding bottles of any region, especially one as new as this, that make the headlines, and no one expects every bottle of red Bordeaux to live up to Cheval Bland '47, nor does anyone complain because the Bordeaux 1977s gave us less than the 1975s. In time we shall learn to recognise the most consistent wineries of Oregon and understand the varying styles and qualities of the vintages just as, in time, we took our fix on other wine regions of the world. It need take no time at all, however, to understand that the Willamette Valley, in common with all climatically marginal wine grape-growing areas, will on occasion produce great wines precisely because it *cannot* guarantee consistency.

As for 'escaping the orbit of the local market', the problem is finding a path to those who might enjoy Oregon wines. Except in the state and in neighbouring Washington, the wines are indeed poorly distributed. Few wineries ship anything at all away from the north-west, and those that do have met choked wholesale systems, overstocked retailers, and consumers indifferent only because, to them, Oregon means nothing more than lumberjacks, Pendleton shirts and ecology. And, to put it bluntly, there is no really large winery in the state to act as a locomotive for others. The three largest, Tualatin, Sokol Blosser and Knudsen-Erath, presently ship fewer than 25,000 cases a year each, and, of that, less than ten per cent of any one of them leaves the north-west. Smaller wineries often have the makeshift air of tight financing, and no one need ask why cultivating the market on their doorstep has been given priority. Of those whose wines are most likely to be available, Tualatin's 1980 Pinot Noir was awarded a trophy at an international competition in London, as was its 1981 Chardonnay. Both varietals are of consistently high quality in later vintages, too, and where dry Gewürztraminer in California is often – how shall I say? – short of breath, Tualatin's is long and elegantly balanced. Sokol Blosser Chardonnays tasted recently included the 1980, 1981 and 1982. Of the three I preferred the last and the first, even though the fruit of the 1980 was beginning to fade and oak to show through. The 1981 showed too much of the citrus nose and flavour associated with the Chardonnay clone 108 developed and distributed by the University of California at Davis, as prevalent in Oregon as it is in California. In California, though, growing conditions make it easier to wrap that lemony note in a way that leaves it less dominant. Robert McRitchie, Sokol Blosser's talented wine maker, seems to have achieved that in Oregon, too, with his 1982. Sokol Blosser's

Rieslings are a trifle sweeter than I would have thought necessary for balance, but they show good, firm character and age well. McRitchie would like to hold the winery's Rieslings longer in bottle before releasing them. The winery's 1983 Pinot Noir was one of the three (along with Yamhill Valley Vineyards and Adelsheim Vineyard) which so impressed the tasters of New York.

In addition to Pinot Noir, Adelsheim Vineyard produces a well-respected Chardonnay, somewhat heavier than usual for the Willamette Valley. 'I make it in a style people are used to', David Adehsheim told me, obviously alluding to some widely appreciated California Chardonnays; 'gradually I shall modify it to a more Oregonian style and hope to take our clientele with us'. I have also enjoyed Pinot Noir from Knudsen-Erath in the past (Dick Erath's 1976 was especially memorable) but I have been less impressed by their wines recently.

Pinot noir and *chardonnay, riesling* and *Gewürztraminer,* and now *pinot gris,* are the varieties that have met with success in Oregon, though a few wineries make excellent wines from other varieties transported from Washington vineyards. (Oregon wineries get very defensive about the use of grapes from across the Columbia river; those who did – almost all of them at one time or another – but no longer need to, take a very holy attitude towards their errant peers, even though wines made from Washington grown grapes are clearly identified as such on the label and help many small wineries to survive economically. They also broaden their scope, because, though to the north, most Washington vineyards are east of the Cascades and in a warmer summer climate where varieties flourish that do less well in Oregon.)

Pinot gris is a comparative newcomer, though David Lett of Eyrie Vineyard, who started it all, now has fourteen acres in production. His 1983, fruity and pebbly, reminded me of the best I have had of this variety in Alsace and in Baden (where it is known as the *Ruländer*). It is full and aromatic, combining qualities of both Burgundy and Alsace. Eyrie Vineyard's Pinot Noir had astonished the French (and upset Robert Drouhin) in those important tastings of 1979 and 1980, and the winery's impeccably balanced Chardonnays, made from vines taken as cuttings from the Draper Ranch on Spring Mountain above Napa Valley, have none of the assertiveness of clone 108.

Myron Redford of Amity Vineyard also has some *chardonnay* vines that originated from Draper Ranch cuttings, and he introduces their grapes judiciously to lots from his clone 108 vines to make sinewy, richly flavoured blends. On his rickety deck, watching the sun settle behind the Coast Range, we ended a Willamette summer day a year ago with a barbecued leg of lamb and his delicious 1979 and 1981 Pinot Noirs. Gazing philosophically at the vineyard falling away beneath us in the gathering dusk of the valley, he confessed that his own presence in Willamette was the result of an accidental chain of events that had started with his eavesdropping on a conversation at the University of Washington's Faculty Club. He agreed that those who had warned of the problems of the Willamette Valley had been right – to a point. 'Fortunately, I knew nothing of all that at the time. Had more of us known it couldn't be done, we might never have done it.'

CHAMPAGNE ANTIQUES

Brian Beet

For those of us unfortunate enough to have been born inveterate collectors but who have also been blessed with a love of wine, the choice of subjects to collect is perhaps too wide. Should we pursue drinking glasses, decanters, corkscrews, labels or any one of several other possible themes? Each of these subjects is wide enough to occupy a lifetime's collecting, not to mention several fortunes. Why not, therefore, build a collection based on a single wine? This would enable the collector to acquire a selection from each of the potential subjects, all grouped around a central theme.

No wine is more suited to such a project than champagne. Not only is the range wider than that for other wines, but the objects tend to be more specific. For instance, it would be difficult to define a burgundy glass but, because of its peculiar properties, champagne inspired specialised tools such as wire nippers and champagne taps. Moreover, because of its timeless image of luxury and extravagance, an amazing range of household and personal accoutrements were made in the form of champagne bottles and corks.

To review the field of champagne accessories it is best to proceed in the order in which they would be used, and start, not unnaturally, in the cellar.

Bin labels for distinguishing the contents of the cellar became necessary towards the end of the eighteenth century as the practice evolved of laying down wine to mature in the bottle. Pottery was always the most popular material and the earlier examples can be found in delftware, creamware and pearlware. Up to about 1870 it is difficult to find labels for individual growths such as Sillery and Ay but, as consumers became more sophisticated in the last quarter of the nineteenth century, larger labels were made, sometimes in wood, which could accommodate full details of shipper and vintage.

The bottle must then be cooled. The individual ice bucket most commonly used today is a relatively modern artefact. Before its advent there were three alternative methods of cooling: a wine cistern, a wine cooler, and a vessel incorporating an ice pocket. The last method will be discussed later under decanters.

A wine cistern is simply a large tub of ice in which several bottles are cooled at a time. Somewhat confusingly, they are frequently referred to nowadays as 'wine coolers'. Made from wood, stone or, much more rarely, silver, they pre-date the invention of sparkling champagne. Being basically pieces of furniture, they follow the fashions of the day and, as with other cooling devices, were obviously intended for all white wines and not just

A wine cooler in old Sheffield plate made about 1810, and a champagne decanter of half bottle size made in 1894. The silver gilt mount incorporates a lock in the lid!

Rare brass champagne cork grip in the form of a bottle of Heidesieck 1893. This device is hollow and fitted with a serrated ring in the base. It is placed over the cork and used to help ease it out 4 inches high.

champagne. In wine coolers proper the ice is packed round a sleeve which accommodates the bottle and is covered by a cowl. This arrangement keeps the bottle dry while simultaneously increasing the insulation of the ice. Almost always intended for single bottles, they were usually manufactured in pairs. They appeared around the beginning of the eighteenth century, when silver was initially the favourite material, to be succeeded by silver plate once a commercial manufacturing process had been developed in the middle of the century.

With the opening of the bottle we come to the first group of objects specific to champagne, although, as with champagne taps, there is some overlap with soda water because of the similarity in early bottling methods. Opening tools fall roughly into three categories: champagne knives, wire nippers and cork grips.

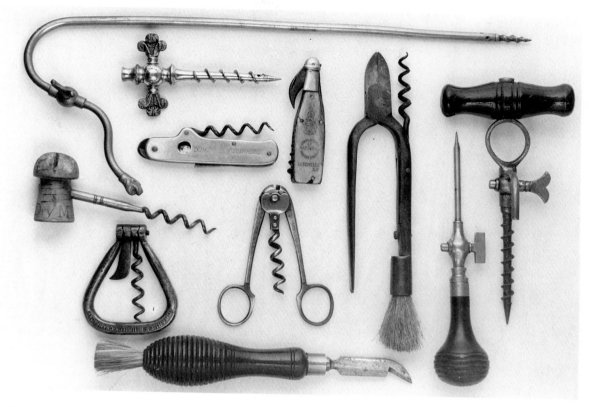

Champagne knives appear at about the beginning of the Victorian era. A wooden handle is fitted at one end with a brush for dusting the bottle, while at the other end a blade protrudes which is serrated for most of its length and ends in a sharpened hook. The hook is used to break the wire or string, and the blade to ease out the cork. Sometimes this arrangement was adapted to form the handle of a corkscrew. As time went by folding pocket varieties evolved and the blade tended to get shorter so that it was intended mainly as a wire breaker, frequently combined with other pocket tools.

Wire nippers come in two basic varieties, pliers and scissors. The plier type often had a brush at the end of one handle and a cork easer on the other. They occasionally incorporated cork grips and, more rarely, a corkscrew. The scissor type was intended for the pocket and was often combined with other aids (cigar cutters being the most common), but again, corkscrew combinations are surprisingly scarce.

Cork grips enabled the cork to be partly eased out and usually consisted of two pivoted handles with inner edges shaped and serrated. More often than not a hook or nippers were provided to deal with the string or wire. Much less often encountered is a circular serrated tool which fitted over the top of the cork, one example of which is known in the form of a champagne bottle.

The bottle opened, there is the option, surprising for many, of decanting the champagne. If performed with a steady hand and into a cool vessel,

A selection of opening tools and champagne taps. The knife at the bottom bears the mark of R Timmins & Sons of Birmingham and appears thus in their trade catalogues from the 1840's.

little mousse is lost, especially if it is consumed within a relatively short time. From the rarity of surviving examples, however, we can assume that this was always a minority practice. Also, there were periodic contributory factors such as the late Georgian prejudice against bottles appearing at table and the late Victorian passion for novelties. There was for a while a social prejudice against wine bottles appearing at table. The most notorious instance of this was the 'Black Bottle' scandal of 1840 when Lord Cardigan put one of his officers on a charge for having a bottle of hock at table during a mess dinner, although contemporary reaction shows that it was felt by then to be an old-fashioned convention.

Decanters generally did not become truly fashionable until the middle of the eighteenth century. Before that all wine was usually served in bottles, sometimes of clear glass. With the advent of decanters, however, two types emerged which were intended specifically for champagne. The first type was engraved with a label for the wine. Engraved label decanters are uncommon, probably because their restrictive use made them less popular, and their use for wine seems to have ceased by the end of the century. Examples for champagne are particularly rare. The second type was a decanter provided with a pocket for ice. These appeared in contemporary bills as 'ice champagne decanters' . From early Victorian times, however, the jug became a more popular receptacle for the ice pocket and appeared in contemporary trade catalogues as a 'champagne jug'. Collectors should not be confused by the large, wide-mouthed jugs with a central cylindrical ice compartment. Although sometimes referred to as champagne jugs today, these were originally intended for lemonade. The end of the nineteenth century saw the introduction of a plain decanter with a silver mount in the form of the cork and foil of a champagne bottle . These were meant to be used in a wine cooler and are an amusing example of the then current fashion for producing everyday objects in novel forms.

Decanter labels, now normally called wine labels, were fully covered by Bernard Watney in *Christie's Wine Companion 2* (1983). Examples for champagne are not common, but by collecting a single wine name the emphasis of a collection will naturally concentrate on the evolution of design, reflecting in microcosm the changing fashions of the ages and frequently displaying a very high degree of craftsmanship. As with bin labels, it is very difficult to find labels for individual growths or distinctions such as 'dry', 'sweet', 'red' or 'white'.

If, following majority practice, the champagne is to be served in the bottle, you may well consider using a bottle holder or a bottle jacket. Bottle holders, which first emerged in the 1860s, consist of a handle which grips the bottle by the neck and the body or base. They preserve the bottle from the heat of the hand and the hand from the cold of the bottle. Bottle jackets are a further sophistication of the idea of completely encasing the bottle to improve insulation. They appear to be a product of the 1880s and, like holders, were almost always made in silver plate .

Now at last the champagne must be drunk and the question of glasses can be considered. The story of the development of design, construction and decoration of drinking glasses is far too complex to be covered here so the discussion will be restricted to the bowl shapes known to have been used for champagne. Suffice it to say that a collection of champagne glasses will encompass all periods of wine-glass making and reflect changing

A bottle jacket in silver plate, made around 1895 by Wm Hutton & Sons of Sheffield.

fashions, so the would-be collector should read a few general books before embarking on the task.

The flute, which pre-dates the arrival of sparkling champagne, seems never to have fallen out of favour and appears in all styles . Surprisingly, it was also the favourite shape for ale glasses until well into the nineteenth century, examples commonly being found engraved with hops and barley. The *coupe* bowl was popular in the first half of the eighteenth century, but its intended use is still a matter of considerable debate, many having rims quite unsuitable for drinking and deemed to have been used for sweetmeats . This shape then virtually disappears until the 1830s when it re-emerges indisputably as a champagne glass. From the outset of its second appearance it was made with a hollow stem which caused a central column of bubbles to effervesce in the middle of the bowl. This hollow stem also occurred with the tulip bowl style later in the century.

1. Champagne ice decanter c.1760, *2.* a tulip bowl glass with opaque twist stem c.1765, *3.* a flute with airtwist stem c.1750, *4* Champagne glass with gadrooned cup-shaped bowl on baluster stem c.1720, *5.* coupe with double ogee bowl on baluster and airbead stem c.1720.

From a drawing by John
Leech in *Punch*.

'Now, George, my boy, there's a glass of Champagne for you. Don't get such stuff at school, eh?'
'H'm! Awfully sweet. Very good sort for ladies. But I've arrived at a time of life when I
confess I like my wine dry.'

A champagne stand in
brass on a wood base,
probably made about 1890
by Farrow and Jackson.

The tulip bowl, which cognoscenti now hold to be the ideal, originated in
the 1760s but is quite rare before late Victorian times. A bowl
shape which might be considered as a foreshortened tulip – like the fat end
of an egg, described by writers on glass as 'cup shaped' – occurs
in the first half of the eighteenth century and was referred to in a bill of 1753
as a champagne glass. This type is also rare, but it must be remembered
that at this time champagne was a very expensive wine and the preserve of
only the truly wealthy. Towards the end of the nineteenth century a small
tumbler made its appearance in suites of table glass. Nowadays called a
'pony' glass, this was consistently described in contemporary trade
catalogues as a 'champagne tumbler'.

Now comes the problem of preserving the remainder of the bottle until
another time. No doubt this strikes many modern day readers as
horrifying, but champagne was considered to have medicinal properties
and doctors would prescribe a glass to be taken once or twice a day. To this
need must be added that of bars and restaurants who wished to dispense
wine by the glass.

Thus was invented the champagne tap. It probably appeared first in
France in 1828, but was certainly in production in Britain from the 1840s.
The basic concept was to drive or screw a tap through the cork without
extracting it, but the Victorian enthusiasm for invention produced a great
variety of different types . In 1868 the bottle stopper emerged which
was screwed onto the neck after the cork had been removed, frequently
also incorporating a tap. Much less seldom encountered is the champagne
stand, a large vice to contain the fizz after opening. From manufacturers'
catalogues we know that these were intended for use in bars wishing to
'keep sparkling wines on draught' and that the more expensive models
held the bottle upside down with a tap in the neck. Little research has been
done into taps and closures so there remains much work to be done and
exciting finds to be made.

With taps we come to the end of the review of champagne accessories and proceed to the subject of champagne-related objects. The principal source of these is the champagne houses and shippers, who produced a wide range of articles bearing their name – often in the form of champagne bottles or corks – as promotional material . These would encompass some of the tools already described, but also articles for bar use such as condiments, bells, menu holders, lighters, match cases, cigar boxes and ashtrays. Similarly, many personal items were made as gifts for favoured customers and, besides opening tools, there are cigar cutters, pocket match cases, pens, propelling pencils, penknives, purses and tape-measures. An interesting collection could be formed of articles bearing the name of a particular house or shipper.

The majority of this promotional material was produced in late Victorian and Edwardian times, a period of peak consumption of champagne in Britain. At this time also there was an enormous vogue for novelties. As has already been stated, the image of champagne was ideally suited to this fashion and articles can be found in the shape of bottles or corks which bear no champagne name and were obviously made just for the fun of it. Articles so far encountered include pepper pots, scent bottles, vinaigrettes, cigarette holders, pipes, inkwells, and seals; but no doubt, as in the other areas, much remains to be discovered.

Two pocket cigar-cutters (design registered in 1882); an American silver plated pocket match case with spring release, in the form of a bottle of 'Duminy'; a plated match case in the form of a crate of Moët (design registered in 1891); a travelling inkwell in the form of a bottle in a cooler; a match case made from an actual Bollinger cork (design registered in 1878).

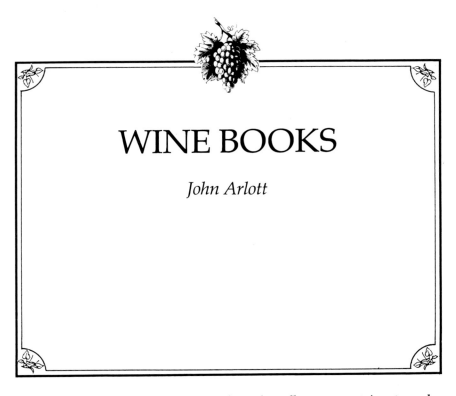

WINE BOOKS

John Arlott

The range of wine books, quite apart from the collector aspect, is extremely far-sweeping: antiquarian, literary, technical, historical, scientific, politically-related, appreciative and financial. Every one of these angles demands a considerable survey few have received, especially in Britain which, despite the plantings of the Romans, still is not truly a wine country, although in recent years consumption and range of experience have certainly increased, if not yet production.

The collecting of wine books has seen a surprisingly healthy and rapid growth in recent years. For example, the 1982 edition of *Which? Wine Guide* listed four wine-book specialists. The 1986 issue notes eleven (covering cookery as well) plus one general bookseller with an appreciable wine section.

Without counting, it has for some time been obvious, even to those without any special interest, that whereas only a few years ago, wine books were not often seen in the shops, they are now quite frequent.

The subject, of course, is of some antiquity. In 1927, André Simon, scholar and collector of wine writings as well as arch-appreciator and missionary-guide to the British people on wine, published *Bibliotheca Bacchica* (reissued 1972 with addenda of twelve titles), listing 711 works on wine published before the year 1600. To be sure they were almost entirely concerned with the growing of vines, some contained only a little on the subject of wine, but they demonstrated the extent of the early, largely technical, literature on the subject.

Incidentally, for the benefit of students anxious for a sight of some of those rarities, many of them came from André Simon's own collection, a substantial proportion of which moved with him to the Wine Trade Club library. When it closed in 1966, a major part of it passed to the library of the Institute of Masters of Wine and has been most valuably catalogued by the

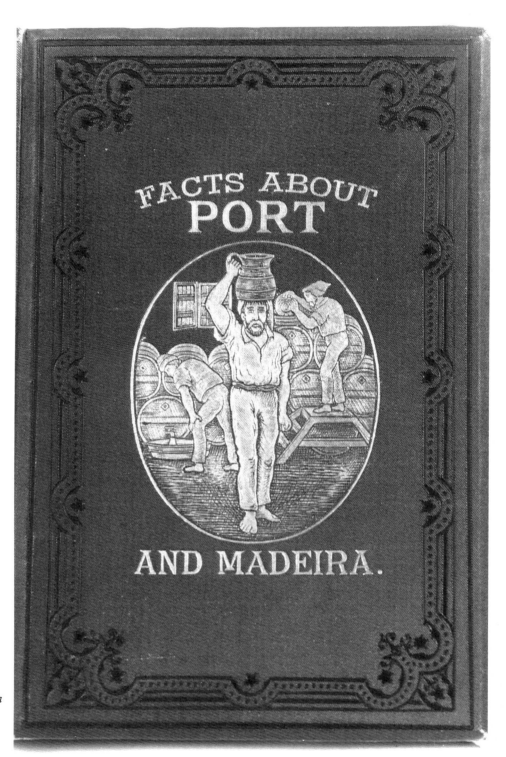

Facts about Port and Madeira
by Henry Vizitelli,
published by Ward Lock,
London, and Scribner,
New York. 1889.

'The Italian Vintage' from the *History and Description of Modern Wines* by Cyrus Redding, published by Bohn, Covent Garden, London. 1851.

London Guildhall library. The early books, of course, were very rarely in English, but generally in the earlier instances in Latin and subsequently in French or Italian.

Apart from the technical/agricultural studies, English wine writing began to develop, though not in any great strength, during the nineteenth century. It is important to realise that in Britain wine drinking was then a class – upper class – matter. There were, however, a few interesting, near-popular publications produced here on the subject in the nineteenth century and into the twentieth: Charles Tovey's four titles, *Wit, Wisdom and Morals Distilled from Bacchus* (1878), *Wine Revelations (1881), Wine and Wine Countries* (1862), and *Champagne, Its History and Manufacture* (1870); Accum's determinedly scientific studies; Cyrus Redding's *History and Description of Modern Wines* (1833) (almost a best-seller in its day); Thomas Shaw's *Wine, the Vine and the Cellar* (1863); Henry Vizetelly's *Facts about Sherry, Facts about Port and Madeira*, and the quite spectacularly period, illustrated *History of Champagne*; the works of the two younger members of the family, *The Wines of France*, carried British wine writing steadily up to the First World War. Still, though, it remained a minority interest.

Then, in 1921, came the highly influential *Notes on a Cellar Book*, by the famous literary historian, Professor George Saintsbury. Opinions about its literary merits and political attitude vary, but there can be no doubt that it had a most considerable effect on the still limited wine literature of Britain.

Another important wine influence of the period was the convivial Charles Walter Berry, wine merchant and occasional essayist (*In Search of Wine, A Miscellany of Wine,* and the slight but memorable *Tokay*). The most influential figure of the inter-war period, however, perhaps in the whole development of wine consciousness in Britain, was the Frenchman, André Simon.

Born in Paris, he came to England at seventeen. His influence on wine drinking in England was to extend over some seventy years. At first he earned his living as the representative of a champagne firm. However, he became quite a considerable scholar on the subject of wine – he wrote, among other studies, a history of the wine trade in Britain – and had an immense missionary urge to preach wine to the British.

A vineyard consultation
from Johann Rasch's
*Weinbuch: Von Baw, Pfleg
vnd Brauch des Weins,*
published by Adam Berg,
Munich. 1582.

Before the First World War he had founded the Wine Trade Institute and written prolifically and informatively, if not always to the highest literary standard, in his adopted language. He was, however, an admirable, generous and quite delightful figure who, in 1933, founded the Wine and Food Society and, indeed, created a world of wine consciousness for many young and some older Englishmen.

Another influential figure of the period was P. Morton Shand whose work in retrospect appears even more impressive than it did at the time. The fact is, and it cannot be too heavily emphasised, that these men were writing for a minority wine audience in a beer (and whisky) drinking community.

It is essential also to realise, yet all too often overlooked, that in the countries which produce wine naturally – and always have done – wine drinking is unselfconscious. That may, interestingly, be the reason why so many people in those countries do not, or used not to, read about drinking wine, as distinct from making it, any more than they read about breathing. To the British, at least to the vast majority of the British, wine drinking became a new and even exciting experience. Whereas an Italian peasant at midday would simply open his unlabelled bottle of wine and with it heighten his bread-and-sausage midday meal, the Englishman increasingly began to read the label and to want to know what it meant. This was a miraculous opportunity for wine writers. After André Simon, Tommy Layton was probably the chief popular inter-war educator; but a growing

List of all wines to be found in Rome, published by Nicholas van Aelst in the early seventeenth century. This may be the oldest wine list.

minority of the British did in fact want to be educated about wine and they turned to the writers to do it for them.

The inter-war period saw growing interest in a few writers of the older school. Their work might be classed as appreciation. It dealt largely with fine wines available only to the wealthy minority: the *grands crus* clarets, the monumental burgundies and the vintage ports. Men like the barrister, Maurice Healy, and the wine merchant, Ian Maxwell Campbell, still wrote for those members of the English upper classes who were drinking ten per cent of the world's finest wine. It was an utter anachronism. Yet for a period it did exist, even flourished, and their writing provides a mirror of that period.

The Second World War was to prove the hinge. It took many British people in the services overseas, where they drank wine, often for the first time. They were the customers awaiting the – coincidentally? – informative work of H. Warner Allen (*A History of Wine*, 1961), Edward Hyams (*Dionysus*, 1965) and William Younger (*Gods, Men and Wine*, 1966). Strangely enough, through all literature, the right writers and books have appeared to meet the demand of history.

This is a socially moulded literature. This was the age of the package holiday, the continental motor tour and, finally, the large scale importation and supermarket sale of wine to a vast new British public.

Of course, immensely serious and original technical books are still being written here, especially on aspects of the newly revived English vine growing and wine making: some of it is highly technical and backed by courses at universities and colleges.

The wider demand has been most handsomely and generously met. First there were the felicitous, historical and appreciation essays of Cyril Ray, the translation of the massive *Encyclopaedia* of Alexis Lichine; the alert appreciations of Jancis Robinson and Pamela Vandyke Price; but latterly and, above all, the work of Hugh Johnson. By the time it went into its third revised edition, his *World Atlas of Wine* had run to an amazing two million copies, selling in many countries and languages. This was the great historic breakthrough: a British wine writer accepted throughout the world of wine. His *Wine Companion* is pressing up behind it. He undoubtedly has something ideal for the English wine reader's mind. A tireless gatherer of facts, he has a virtually encyclopaedic gift for arrangement. There is little doubt that he has reinforced to an immense degree the British interest in, and demand for, wine books. Perhaps, indeed, we should not be surprised to find English wine writing accepted outside Britain. After all, the first version of *Bordeaux and Its Wines*, later to become known as 'Cocks et Feret', was written solely by the Englishman, Charles Cocks, in English, and published by an English firm. Cocks was highly knowledgeable on the subject, and virtually anticipated the classification of 1855. His publisher, Feret, added his name to the second edition; and now Cock's credit has been deleted altogether. Fittingly, though, that fine scholar of wine, Edmund Penning-Rowsell, has established his *The Wines of Bordeaux*, edition by edition, as authoritative. Similarly, Michael Broadbent, the most widely translated and published expert on tasting, has produced a *magnum opus* in his *Great Vintage Wine Book*. Latterly there has even been an intrusion of humour into English wine writing – a degree of sophistication which must have seemed utterly impossible only a few years ago – and it was all given a fresh twist by Simon Loftus's perceptive and witty *Anatomy of the Wine Trade*.

It has not only become an emancipated literature, but it has increasingly opened booksellers' doors to continental writers. Many of the books now coming on to the British – and French and United States – markets might be described as 'coffee table'; certainly the subject has proved as photogenic as that of cuisine. Publishers, notably Mitchell Beazley who produced the *World Atlas*, have moved adventurously and seriously into the wine-book market. Meanwhile, the booksellers have sensed their opportunity. The wine-book collector can now move far back in time – where he will pay some fairly horrifying sums, for few bought as André Simon did – or create a new, informed and interesting library of modern books. The growth of the Australian and Californian wine industries has been paralleled by the growth in wine drinking and wine reading in Britain. America, of course, has long been, by modern standards, in the field of fine wine: their outstanding books are by Leon D. Adams *(The Wines of America)* and M. A. Amerine *(Wine)*. In Australia, Len Evans has produced a huge, ambitious, authoritative and handsome *Complete Book of Australian Wine,* and James Halliday a series of regional studies. While introducing a fairly fresh area, Frank Thorpy is the author of a substantial history – *Wine in New Zealand.*

There are, too, dealers in wine prints and artefacts, relatively scarce as the latter may be, but they do indicate a new direction for the British collector.

IT TAKES ONE TO KNOW ONE

Nathan L Chroman

In America over the last decade or two, a phenomenon known as a wine boom has occurred wherein the 'grape' has become a fashionable new taste toy. More Americans than ever before have turned to wine for pleasure, status, perhaps a bit of one-upmanship, or simply as a lighter, less spirited alternative to whisky, affectionately referred to in drinking circles as 'booze'.

The decline of 'booze' consumption resulted in Americans taking up with the corkscrew and glass with a vengeance. With Yankee know-how or ignorance, depending upon your point of view, they drank and read everything in sight to compensate for a generation of legally imposed, forced abstinence during the period of Prohibition following the First World War.

Whether or not America is enjoying a wine boom or a 'boomlet' of significant proportion, one aspect is abundantly clear: seasoned wine drinkers and neophytes alike are sniffing, sloshing, swallowing and spitting wine with an unpractised eye and palate towards making a judgment, an organoleptic examination if you will (in case you forgot, the evaluation of wine through the use of one's own senses, ascribing to each perception a quantum of numerical points, the total of which constitutes a good, bad or indifferent wine). Maligned and abused, the technique more often than not suffers from the failure to apply common taste sense (pun intended) arising out of long standing, hard to obtain, critical judging experience.

Daily, as more Americans total organoleptic scorecards, even more endeavour to lay claim to the title of 'wine judge'. Indeed, everyone and his imbibing neighbour are now wine judges, never mind that there are degrees of tasting training, experience and exposure. No taster worth his weight in high-styled claret can be an honest-to-goodness wine judge

...The Chairman reviews notes
of the Grignolino panel.

...The wine author
takes a break.

unless his palate has seriously and deliberately touched a goodly quantity of wine, say a thousand bottles or so. Now is that asking too much for such a time-honoured vaunted title? No, considering the endlessly boring vacuous taste pronouncements we all hear these days across the table, from a wine pulpit and the wine press.

Whether competent or not, wine judging, professionally rendered and organised or not, is an inescapable consequence of more people taking to the grape. Also, it is not simply a matter of 'judges' edicts, but a question of others slavishly following in typical, blind-leading-the-blind, style. No doubt it is a 'catch 22' situation which may not destroy wine and vine *à la phylloxera*, but conceivably could come close.

Since wine judges are now born at the drop of a cork, wine judgings, like young vigorous prolific vines, have multiplied in bunches, so much so that no respectable American metropolis would be caught dead without one. In California city, county and regional fair competitions alone there are at least thirty and, since these comments, there must be a dozen or more arising out of somebody's need and ego to form another. Don't get me wrong, in some cases the cause may be genuine, but in most others it is a self-aggrandising opportunity for many to 'officialise' the title of wine judge.

What's more, vintners throughout the country have compounded the problem by submitting good, bad and generally indifferent wine for award consideration anywhere at any time. It has got so bad that if three wine guzzling Dobermans offered a Thoroughbred's Gold Cup wine award, no doubt wineries would rush to participate. Many vintners, especially new ones, believe they have to play gold medal catch-up to older, traditional established vineyards whose reputations apparently are settled. The best and speediest consumer identification, they argue, is to win a medal, no

... First day, Chardonnay tasting panel. Flight Number One.

... A chewy cabernet.

matter from where, just as long as wineries can brandish an award or two. These days, not having an award is akin to not having wine in the bottle. Marketing techniques, however academically or commercially considered, have fallen to one simple bottom line: how many awards has the winery won lately?

Time was, immediately after Prohibition, there were only two major wine competitions in America. The Los Angeles County Fair judging, composed largely of so-called amateur palates, and the California State Fair competition, administered principally by those with academically trained palates from the Department of Enology and Viticulture of the University of California at Davis. The former required no palate testing while the latter mandated an exam emphasising perception of such basics as sugar, acidity, varietal types, etc. What was fascinating was that frequently the results were similar.

My own tasting experience has been with the Los Angeles County Fair during the late 50s and early 60s when it was chaired by Harold Richardson, a crusty, no-nonsense lawyer who excelled in bringing good palates together for a two-day competition utilising sixteen judges in panels of four. Upon his death in 1967, I assumed the chairmanship (and hold it still) with I hope equal fervour, dedication and a modicum of success.

During the early years, after Prohibition and even into the late 60s, wines were entered by the wineries voluntarily (and neither purchased nor selected by the Fair); there were generally under 200 entries ranging from dry to sweet, sparkling, brandy and even such popular 'vinous concoctions' as chocolate and garlic. Today the judging extends for four days, employing over forty judges who plough through in excess of 2,000 wines.

In those earlier, simpler, primitive, competitions, wines were served to

"... reacting to a
young Reisling,
Monterey County."

each judge by a co-panelist, who poured from an entry bottle covered by a paper bag container with a code name, and type description. An insidious judging problem was that the bags were never sufficiently large to cover the neck and top of the bottle, which, when exposed, would reveal whether it was a cork-finished bottle, or screw-capped. Popular-priced volume, low-end wines were largely topped with screw-caps and generally represented 100,000 cases or more of assembly line production. Actually, it is the kind of wine I enjoyed during my law school salad days; that is heavy, coarse, robust reds. Need it be said which wines generally won awards?

Fortunately, upon my chairmanship, with the help of additional wine stewards, I abrogated the practice and required the wine to be poured into glasses bearing code letters, away from the view of the judges. This forced reliance on palate evaluation rather than on cork-finished prejudice as well as overall greater and better judging reflection. Whether it made judgments more accurate and valid is a question I leave for others.

In any event, the validity of judgments is an impossible determination. Who is to say who or what is correct? Was the nefarious 1976 Paris judging between Californian and French wine an appropriate forum to ascertain which wines were better? Frankly, I wonder about the advisability of such apples-v-oranges competitions. Even at our judging – where wines of the same origin and class, say Cabernet Sauvignon three years old or under, are judged by four judges working six to eight hours per day, starting at 7.00 am and spending two days, possibly three, before the first ranking, much less the final judgment, is made – how reliable are those judgments if there is no accurate measure for judging the judges?

I am not persuaded by testing procedures for the simple reason that the key factors are not taken into consideration. Some judges can judge one glass of wine, another twenty, others forty, and make sensible and, one hopes, accurate judgments, while others are numb after a taste or two. Moreover, what is the value of identifying basic components such as sugar and acid if Cabernet is not accurately identified and understood, especially considering the variety of styles from across such a large viticultural region as California? Cabernet from Mendocino County to the north of California is decidedly distinct from Cabernet in Sonoma, Santa Clara and, some 400 miles down the road from Napa to Santa Barbara, the wines are yet again dramatically different. Whose Cabernet is best? Whose style is to be the winner?

The question of style is critical. One palate may favour the robust, while the other the mellow. Another question is whether a wine judge can qualify for a California competition if he has not also tasted the wines of the world? Is there merit in an opinion from one without the benefit of long-term cellaring of mature and complex wines as well as those of youth and vigour. Does it not all boil down, then, to a judge who has experience, exposure, opportunity, love, curiosity and the will to taste deliberately daily in an organised manner, even if it is only at table. Tasting four to eight Cabernets a day prior to dinner, day in and day out, may be sufficient to earn a place at the Cabernet judging table. In any case, it is persuasive.

While the search continues for the perfect judge to render an even more perfect judgment, those entrusted with competitive judgment-making events will just have to continue as best they can, perhaps on four cylinders instead of six. To do so in Los Angeles, I have established a coterie of judges whose opinion I respect even though our palates may disagree, but what has been mystifying and fascinating to me is how these judges fall into certain types and styles, much like the wines they judge.

Of course, the common denominator that unifies the judges is the grape, yet there are heated tableside battles reflecting all of humanity's basic characteristics and frailties. Wine judging together with a group of four panellists brings out the worst and the best of these to such an extent that it is impossible for me as a judging administrator to draw any firm, compelling, underlying conclusions. The best I can do is to mention some of the recognisable types which no doubt the reader has encountered too.

Most obvious and largest in number is the prejudiced palate who, no matter the taste and style of a wine or the responsible opinion of others, will cling tenaciously to a judgment even after two to four days of competition protocol. There is no changing of the mind here or even a hint of compromise; the prejudiced palate knows best, and no one should dare challenge. Every competition has a number of these and heaven preserve us from this righteous 'all-knowing' judge.

.. assessing the character of two closely matched sauvignon blanes.

I must confess some guilt in the matter of possessing a prejudiced palate. I recall at my début judging experience I observed a cork-finished bottle rising over the crest of the bag-container and quickly decided that the wine entry, a Johannisberg Riesling, was Stony Hill, a prized tiny winery of no more than fifteen hectares in the Napa Valley. To my co-panelist, I insisted the wine deserved a gold medal and refused to listen even to a plea for modification or reconsideration. The more insistent the plea, the angrier I became. I was immovable. The battle lines were drawn and the impasse was fixed. To clear the air, our panel retired from the judging premises for casual conversation and relaxation. After ten minutes another judge, independent of my panel, brought a glass of wine for me to taste and solicited an opinion, and by that time I was feeling good and confident. Freely and instantaneously, I rendered my judgment and can't you guess which one wine it was? Yes, it was the Stony Hill poured from the very same bottle. I had volunteered that the wine was atrocious and did not belong in the competition. My face was red for weeks, perhaps years thereafter, as my palate became less strident less firmly entrenched in prejudice and more pliable like ageing, silky, supple, claret. While I believe I have been cured, I have not been able to reform those whose irrevocable, irreconcilable judgments have not as yet been humbled by blind tastings.

Another judge type is the European wine fancier who believes the sun rises and sets on the wines of France, Germany, Italy, Spain and Portugal. I can still hear a model prototype judge of this type as he attacked his fellow judges in the Johannisberg Riesling category because none of the California JRs measured up to the German variety. In other words, he was saying we must conform to the likes of the Rhine and under no circumstances should the quality and style of a California JR be taken into consideration. This can be the most dangerous of judges since chauvinism for older traditional regions is often an easy crutch designed to avoid the basic question of wine quality, irrespective of origin.

.. contemplating a potential medal winner.

Indecision is a frequently found characteristic. A noted wine judge several years ago kept a panel for three days on one category just because he could not make up his own mind. Taste after taste was made until he may have looked at the same wine half a dozen or more times and still could not come to grips with what the wine was saying. His argument was that justice grinds slowly, and he would rather not make a mistake in a bad judgment. As a result, he made no judgment. This prompted not a few veteran vintners to claim, with straight faces, that this may have been the best judgment of all.

Those with academically trained palates have their problems too. While most are wine talented, many, with years of laboratory in-depth palate experience, never seem to favour a specific wine. The game plan is to perceive a flaw, seize on it and no matter how the wine may otherwise taste, even like God-given nectar, it is reduced to common, ordinary, even unsound status. While these kinds of palate triumph in the laboratory in wine-making advancement, they often fail to enjoy the sheer pleasure of wine drinking. After all, a flaw is a flaw is a flaw.

Further on the same academic road, newly graduated, academically trained palates do not have the catholic in-depth wine exposure to the world's wine. Limitations of time and income preclude wide experience, which raises an interesting question: can a person exposed only to flawed wine be asked to judge fine ones? Does not the experience of old and young, simple, and complex wines make for a more competent wine judge, notwithstanding academic discipline? My feeling is yes it does, but, of course, at LA it is not as critical since we rely on consensus judgment of panels that are balanced with amateurs and professionals.

Perhaps the most boring judges are the long-winded variety, who, after an initial taste, lecture incessantly on not only what the wine should taste like, but also on what side of the vineyard hill the best wine is likely to come from, and at which moment of the day, during a critical harvest, grape picking should begin. Only after what sounds like ten pages of lecture is the final Solomon-like judgment made and, if not heeded, the pulpit-like lecture is resumed with a final admonition, 'next time read before you taste'. The pearls of wisdom flow like volume wine. I suppose the other panellists should be grateful.

Political conflicts and civil rights debates do not escape the wine judges' discourse even during the heat of competition. One judge would always characterise another's judgment by the colour of his politics. Are you shocked? Believe me it happens. 'Show me what a man thinks politically and I'll tell you what his taste is', said one judge, who generously volunteered a wine politics colour guide: pink for liberals, red for communists, white for pacifists, and light amber and pale-colour brandies for conservatives. Such a judge will request to be seated with a panellist with like politics and refuse association with any displaying a hint of liberality. How politics ever enter into the realm of wine judging is beyond me, but nevertheless it does, to the raging consternation of this writer.

America's women's liberation movement, 'women's lib', has also found its way to our judging tables. During the competition's formative years and on into the 60s, few, if any, women were selected as judges, not because they were incompetent but because principally, and especially in California, very few were available. It was hard enough to find men, much less the few women who took wine seriously but never ventured beyond their own dining room, to express a well-reasoned wine opinion. Surely their husbands were not eager to hear it, much less respect it? I doubt if there was more than one female wine maker then, nor were there many graduates from UC Davis, Department of Enology. Today, there are many with palates who have wine making as well as wine tasting experience who are the envy of their male contemporaries.

While I enjoyed the search and the recruiting of the many women who have sinced judged at the LA competition, there are still those who crusade for the 'lib' movement at the wine judging tables. For one in particular, if the three male co-panellists disagreed with her judgment, it wasn't a question of wine dispute, it was a matter of not respecting (at long last) a woman's wine opinion. Several not so ladylike women judges said loudly and clearly that they would give no quarter in judging discussions, for their palates were free at last!

Wine judges in groups also show prejudices. Take the last competition when all of the panellists, approximately forty, engaged in a serious discussion of taste and style over a Pinot Noir. Apparently, the wine under scrutiny was enthusiastically embraced by the amateur judges' group because of its French-like burgundian style, but spiritedly disdained by the academic judging community for its wine spoilage organism known as brettanomyces. This is a cellar problem that purports to give a wine an aroma not unlike that of a sweaty horse or an old seasoned barn. Frequently found in Burgundy, it is obviously taboo in the wine laboratory.

Each group was certain of its position and neither desired a compromise. One amateur wine judge, said, 'If this is what fine styled Pinot Noir burgundy smells and tastes like, then we should encourage it'. In response a Davis professor threw up his hands and stared at the judge in disbelief. Who is right and who is wrong and do questions like this help in the resolution of the continuing question of wine judge qualification?

Have you found yourself in these few categories of wine judge types? If you do, don't worry, they represent a mirror of wine judges and drinkers everywhere. Qualifying the most competent and best judge is a task for another generation or two, or perhaps, the test-tube creations of outer space and other planets. In the interim, all of us involved in wine competitions will plod along as best we can with the imperfect judge. Indeed, I can scarcely wait for the next competition when I am certain to be confronted and beleaguered by each of my all too human judges with that tired, yet valid cliché, 'it takes one to know one'.

... encountering a happy
little zinfandel from
Amador County.

ON THE ROAD TO ORANGE

Steven Spurrier

'Avignang, Avignang, deux minutes d'arrêêêt!' Your train has arrived in Avignon, and if you haven't been looking out of the window, the accent from the loudspeaker tells you that you're in Provence. The reason for being there is the Foire d'Orange, which is held on the last Saturday in January. It is the earliest and the smallest of the three major French wine-judging fairs of Paris, Mâcon and Orange, and the one I would least wish to miss. If the Foire d'Orange did not exist, a group of us would have had to invent it.

I first went to the Foire d'Orange in 1969, having left the London wine trade a year before, married and retired to the south of France. The trade would soon get me back, but for the moment I was frustrated at being out of it and out of touch, and had never been to a wine fair before except for the grandly organised Hospices de Beaune. The 'fair' part is a week-long exhibition of wine-making equipment, whereas what interested me is the comparative judging of several hundred wines from dozens of *appellations*. In the late 1960s, the judging took place in the Roman arena in the centre of Orange, a splendid site for tasting four-month old wines, and was exclusively local. I brazened my way in, flourishing my passport at the organisers, pointing proudly to my profession described as 'wine merchant', which impressed them enough to put me on a jury tasting Tavel rosé. (Two weeks later in Paris, when applying for a resident's permit to enable me to open a wine shop, I was advised to put *commerçant* as my profession and not *marchand de vin*, a job considered then by the Prefecture de Police as carrying the same social weight as a petrol pump attendant.) My grandfather left England only once and, being passportless, found it entirely sufficient to announce to the foreign police that he was a member of Boodle's. Anyway my British passport and 'wine merchant' got me in, and I have been going back every year since.

From a Paris wine merchant's point of view, the Foire d'Orange is the first and last glimpse of sun for months and a welcome break from stock-taking. For the first few years, I used to go alone, taking the Trans-European Express fittingly called le Mistral – and rent a car in Avignon. This marvellous train left Paris at 1.15 pm and wise travellers reserved their places in the dining car in advance. The entire train was *première classe avec supplement,* but without a lunch reservation one was shuttled into a less comfortable carriage, having been forced to choose between first or second sittings. In the real *wagon-restaurant,* an aperitif was available before the train even left the Gare de Lyon and one never had to leave one's armchair-like seat. Lunch was expensive, but *le grand service*

The Rhône valley in spring is a mass of fruit blossom when the vines have only just begun to sprout.

Tain and the Hill of Hermitage which is alone allowed to call its wines Hermitage.

lasted until Dijon three hours later. On arrival in Avignon, six and a half hours from Paris, there was just time to unpack before dinner at that superb restaurant Hiély. By the mid-1970s, my staff in Paris had grown and we all used to go down by car, saving the price of le Mistral, and spending it on restaurants on the way. The disadvantage was the drive back to Paris on Sunday. Recently, life on the Paris-Avignon run has been considerably eased by the existence of the TGVs, the superb and highly subsidised *trains-à-grande vitesse*.

The actual tasting at Orange lasts only two hours on the Saturday morning, but it is the centrepiece around which plans are made. Everybody from the southern Rhône is there, plus a few from the north and from Provence. The English crowd is much in evidence (including a smattering of MWs) and there is a certain amount of jockeying for position over the wines one is to taste. Here, I have lately adopted a pose of lofty indifference, oblivious to the ignominity of being allotted Côtes de Luberon rosé while my colleagues are given Châteauneuf-du-Pape, for I know that my loyalty and tenacity have been rewarded at the Foire de Mâcon; tasting grands Bourgognes rouges in the comfort and security of Salle No. 1. The important thing at Orange is not to be browbeaten by one's fellow jury members and to have a good luncheon invitation to look forward to afterwards.

This time I planned my trip as carefully as ever with Isabelle Bachelard, of l'Académie du Vin and James Lawther of the Caves de la Madeleine. We left on Thursday's early TGV arriving in Dijon in time to collect our car and be in Gevrey-Chambertin by 9.15, where we were joined by Graham Chidgey of Layton's. We spent the day tasting some superb 1985s at the Domaines Rebourseau and Roumier and some rather tannic older wines at the Domaine des Varoilles and P. Misserey, before leaving the Côte-de-Nuits for the Cortons and Corton-Charlemagnes of Bonneau de Martray and the Pommard Clos des Epeneaux of le Comte Armand. This was punctuated by a sustaining lunch at the Rotissérie de Gevrey-Chambertin. Friday saw us marvelling at the wines, but not the prices, of Pierre Morey in Meursault, confirming our meagre reservation *chez* Blain-Gagnard in Chassagne and leaving Graham Chidgey to the rest of the

Côte-de-Beaune, while we went to lunch with Aubert and Pamela de Villaine in Bouzeron. It was by now snowing hard, and Aubert has the coldest cellars in Burgundy after le Comte Lafon, so we rushed through the 1985s – the best Aubert says he has ever made – to get to lunch in the kitchen. My palate was in such good shape that I missed the vintage of 'an old la Tâche from an unfashionable year' by two decades, picking out the 1954 as a 1974. Thus refreshed (with Aubert attempting to make coffee without boiling the water) we left for the Beaujolais.

Provence starts at Mâcon. After Mâcon, red Roman roof tiles replace the grey slate of the frozen north. My favourite family in the Beaujolais is that of Pierre Ferraud, my main supplier for Paris from this region, whose wines I first got to know in Belleville-sur-Sâone one evening some years ago by drinking my way through half bottles of all the nine crus de Beaujolais (having begun with Mâcon blanc and Beaujolais-villages, at the Hotel le Beaujolais in Belleville-sur-Sâone). Although I had my wife to help with this task, my enthusiasm must have caused some attention, for the following morning Pierre Ferraud stopped by to meet the person who had been involved in such extensive research, and invited us to his cellars across the street. This time we just (this is beginning to sound like Jennifer's or Harry Waugh's diary) managed to taste the 1985s, which I ordered to be bottled in magnums, before rushing off to Ampuis for the beginning of The Real Thing.

Since Marcel Guigal's purchase last year of the venerable firm of Vidal-Fleury a few yards from his own cellars, Guigal-Fleury is probably the only reason to stop in Ampuis. Marcel is very serious about his wines and has become almost God-like in his pronouncements: 'We do not go to Orange to taste; we have never done so, it is too early.' His preference for dark-coloured, intense wines is plain; even his Côtes du Rhône is extraordinary: 'twenty per cent Syrah, twenty-five per cent Mourvèdre, ten per cent Counoise and forty-five per cent of the lesser varieties', quotes Marcel, thus dismissing Grenache and Cinsault, the mainstay of wines from the southern Rhône. The special *cuvées* of la Mouline and La Landonne are the equal of any wine in France, to which he has added a third from 1985, 'La Turque' from the Vidal-Fleury vineyards. At Guigal's we were joined by Jean-Marie Picard, from whom I recently bought a bar on the left bank in Paris. This has enabled him to set up in great style an hotel-restaurant at Malataverne, lost in the vineyards outside Montélimar. Also present was an Australian lady, Minty Lalanne, with whom we were to spend the night.

Minty's house is hidden in the hills above Vaison-la-Romaine, part of the ancient Enclave du Pape, a triangle of the three villages of Vaison, Visan and Vinsobres, referred to locally as *le triangle du vice*. It is very beautiful, simple, the heart of la France Profonde, with unspoilt views over to Monte Ventoux and the Luberon. It is the perfect place in which to wake up at the start of an arduous day's tasting in Orange.

The tasting takes place in the Salle des Fêtes on the outskirts of the town (which doubles up as an auction house for cattle and agricultural produce). Juries are made up of four people, two from the region and two 'foreigners', one of whom is usually non-French. The thirty or so wines per table, selected according to category and *appellation*, are judged as being medal worthy or not, and then rejudged for the appropriate medals. In recent years the quality seems to have risen as the generosity of the tasters

The vines in the Côte
Rôtie cling to steep slopes
which run right down to
the Rhône.

has declined. All the wines are, of course, tasted blind and the results are
announced at the end of the lunch that follows. We avoid this lunch, as it
takes up too much valuable time. My team, and the rest of the Mafia
Anglais in Paris (which is made up of people who used to work for me and
who have now gone into co-operative competition with me) always leave
for the Château de Beaucastel, owned by the Perrin family. François Perrin,
the younger son, is in charge of the vines and shares the final wine-making
decisions with his brother Jean-Pierre. The tasting starts with white
Châteauneuf-du-Pape, both tank fermented and barrel-fermented. The
whites always end with an oddity. This time it was a late-harvest
Châteauneuf, picked on December 10 after a fall of snow, which was
luscious and heavily perfumed, more like a Tokay d'Alsace than anything
else, which François had made *pour s'amuser*. Once on the reds, we begin
with the seven major varieties that make up a good Châteauneuf
(Beaucastel has the full thirteen varieties, both red and white, one of only
two *domaines* to do so), which nobody gets right, but where the Mourvèdre
usually stands out, bettering even the Syrah. François then makes an
off-the-cuff blend which surpasses the individual parts. After looking at a
few older wines, we go upstairs for lunch. This year, François and his wife
had laid on a buffet. Lunch is all home made, bought at the market that
morning and quite delicious. It is also a time of danger, for there is more

tasting to be done in the afternoon. Too much Beaucastel at lunch induces in this writer what John Livingstone-Learmonth refers to as *le pli* (the collapse, or fold).

Our first post-lunch appointment is with Monsieur Reynaud at Château Rayas, for which we are late but not folded. Monsieur Reynaud *fils* is an eccentric (his equally eccentric father died at a great age in 1978), who maintains an *encépagement* containing the disallowed *chardonnay* and *pinot noir* grapes, and who makes his wine in a cellar of extreme rusticity. He wears a beret Basque and thick spectacles, behind which sparkle brown eyes of sardonic intelligence. He is the only *vigneron* I have ever seen taste his wines directly from the pipette. Since these wines are very desirable and in short supply and Jacques Reynaud only sells to people who he thinks

Old vines surrounded by the enormous pebbles which absorb the heat of the sun. In the background the Dentelles de Montmirail.

understand them, tasting well is rewarded with the possibility of having an order accepted, so it is advisable to keep *le pli* until later.

Later, we were on our way back to Vaison-la-Romaine by way of Gigondas. Monsieur Roger Meffre, of the Domaine Saint Gayan, is president of the Foire, and had given us a rendezvous *après le déjeuner, vers 5.30*. We arrived almost on time and tasted everything he had, from a Côtes du Rhône 1985 to a magnificent Gigondas 1981. The mistral had been blowing for some days, so the *chais* and cellars were icy, but this alone does not affect one's ability to taste. Taste buds are hampered by the vast amount of tannin in these wines, which leaves one's mouth and tongue black and the jaws clamped tightly together. After mumbling goodbye to Monsieur Meffre, we drove up the hill to see the Roux brothers of the Domaine des Pallières, which is perhaps the most traditional of all Gigondas properties. Their current vintage is 1982. At this stage in the day, the plummy 1985 tasted better than the mature 1982, so it was time to stop. On the way back to Vaison, we bought some aromatic and soothing Condrieu and some under-priced Hermitage from Delas and dined in, chez Madame Lalanne.

The following day, we had expected an early appointment with Alain Roux at the Château du Trignon in Sablet, but this was cancelled, as his premises were occupied by the buyers from the *Sunday Times* Wine Club. That left us with just an easy tasting of beautifully made Vins du Pays du Vaucluse and Côtes du Rhône at the Domaine du Vieux Chêne at Camaret, before embarking on the final excitement, lunch at Hiély in Avignon.

Hiély is one of the greatest restaurants in France, and has had two stars in the Michelin guide for ever. I first went there in 1961, when the set menu cost 12.50 francs. It is now 220 francs and very good value indeed. The cuisine is mainly regional and most inventive; the wine list is heavy in the best local wines at honest prices. The restaurant is on the first floor, which helps to impart a sense of peace, expectation and unhurried gastronomy that is rivalled, in my experience, only by Taillevent. It is also, like Taillevent, a restaurant where having a good meal, beautifully served with appropriate wines, is the only important thing. The four of us had a splendid time, all ordering different things and digging into each other's plates. We drank Châteauneufs, both white and red, and followed these with 1985 Côtes du Rhône *en carafe*, which shocked nobody. James and I left to catch the Sunday afternoon TGV, leaving Minty and Isabelle to their ice-creams, and arrived in Paris a few beers and a little under three and a half hours later. Getting from Paris to London took a little longer.

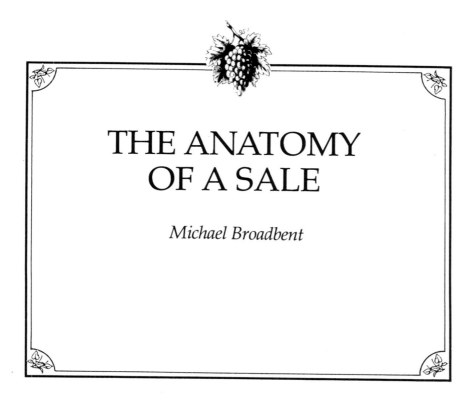

THE ANATOMY OF A SALE

Michael Broadbent

'Charlie, I would like you to meet Michael Broadbent, the head of our new wine department.' This brief introduction took place just twenty years ago, in the early autumn of 1966. 'Charlie' turned out to be the Marquis of Linlithgow. He was introduced by Patrick Lindsay, a colleague and senior partner of Christie's. During the course of a brief chat Lord Linlithgow casually mentioned that he and his brother were tired of dipping into their stock of eighteenth-century madeira: some bottles were nice but some were not, so they just threw the bottles away. I gulped hard and asked, in my most diffident manner, if I could possibly come and see the family cellar.

A week or so later I took a train to Edinburgh and dined early with an old school friend who then kindly drove me out of the city, towards the Forth Bridge, and up the long, imposing drive to Hopetoun House. It was a dark October evening and, having climbed the broad flight of steps to the front door, I took some time to find anything which resembled a bell or knocker. Finally the door was opened to reveal his lordship and the butler, the latter struggling to put on his black jacket, my host still sporting scarlet-coloured felt braces. They had both been watching the Miss World contest on their respective television sets. I had timed it beautifully and they were comparing notes.

The thing I was soon to learn about the aristocracy was that they are relaxed and easy. They have no 'side'. It is the upwardly mobile or static middle classes who furnish this world with snobs. Anyway, a glass of whisky and a chat by the fireside were followed by bed and anything but a sound sleep. I read *My Life and Loves* by Frank Harris.

The next morning I was guided down to the cellars which, as so often in big houses, were beneath the flagged main hall, and with pad in hand I took stock, working methodically from top left to bottom right, one wall of bins after another. There were the old madeiras, and claret, port,

Mentmore near Aylesbury.

champagne and liqueurs, all lightly dust covered and clearly bin labelled. One bin was full of the rare 1911 Coronation vintage of Sandeman's.

Just as I was leaving the house Lord Linlithgow mentioned casually that Harry Rosebery 'across the road' was 'getting on' and had a lot of old claret that he would probably like to get rid of. He slipped a scrap of paper into my hand which turned out to be a rough list of a most extraordinary collection of pre-phylloxera claret. It was mostly Lafite – 'Harry's father was a Rothschild you know' – and the final tip was not to be too modest when estimating the sale prices. Since the new wine department had not sold a serious collection of pre-phylloxera claret before, and as Christie's pre-war price records were clearly out of date, it was really very difficult to say what, for example, a magnum of 1864 Lafite would fetch at auction just over a century after it was made.

I wrote to Lord Rosebery and made an appointment to visit Dalmeny, a dark brooding house surrounded by its own private golf course in a huge park overlooking the Firth of Forth.

The butler conducted me down to an immaculately maintained cellar. It was in two sections with a neat decanting table near the door. The walls

CATALOGUE OF

Finest and Rarest Wines from Private Cellars

including
XVIII century Canary, Hock, Cape wine and Milk Punch;
early and mid XIXth century wines and spirits; Lafite
1858, 1864, 1865, 1870, 1871, 1874, 1878 and 1893.

The Properties of
The Most Honourable The MARQUESS OF LINLITHGOW
The Right Honourable The EARL OF ROSEBERY, K.T.
Amiya, Dowager COUNTESS OF SANDWICH
The Right Honourable The LORD BRUNTISFIELD
COLONEL IAN ANDERSON
MAJOR J. C. F. MAGNAY
MRS. V. A. WATNEY
and others

which will be sold at Auction by
CHRISTIE, MANSON & WOODS, LTD.
Incorporating W. & T. Restell

I. O. CHANCE, J. A. FLOYD, A. G. GRIMWADE, GUY HANNEN, M.C. THE HON. PATRICK LINDSAY,
JOHN HERBERT, A. J. H. DU BOULAY THE HON. DAVID BATHURST, DAVID CARRITT, W. A. COLERIDGE

at their Great Rooms
8 King Street, St. James's London S.W.1
On <u>Wednesday</u> May 31, 1967 at ten-thirty a.m. precisely

Rare bottles from the famous sale held on 28 May 1967.

162 Extrait d'Absinthe

140 Old Hock, about 1780

141 Cape Wine, 1801

129 Canary, 1740

137 Cape Wine from Holland, 1757

130 Milk Punch, 1750

148 Malaga, about 1810

and ceiling were of stone, the floor had a thick layer of gravel and the bin shelves were, I think, of slate. I shall never forget the big bottles: rows of dumpy double-magnums of 1865 Lafite which reminded me of my service in the Royal Artillery. They looked like howitzer shells! None of the old claret was labelled. It was identified, as is customary, by bin labels and cellar books. The latter had been meticulously kept by several generations of Dalmeny butlers. Incidentally, it was the first earl who is reputed to have sent a telegram to one of these butlers: 'I leave for Dalmeny tomorrow. Lady Rosebery and the other heavy baggage will follow.'

On this visit I had the car and a supply of cartons. I packed as much as I could of the oldest and best and drove eagerly but anxiously down the A1 to London, hoping that no one would run into the back of me – unlikely, as my passengers know, unless stationary at traffic lights.

But the job was not over, for I still had the cellars at Mentmore to do. It was here, at the extraordinary 'pile' near Aylesbury, that I met Lord Rosebery for the first time. What first caught my eye was the huge table in the front hall with all his lordship's hats and walking sticks laid out in orderly rows.

The cellar seemed miles away, and was far bigger than that at Dalmeny. I spent all morning underground and broke for lunch. This also I shall never forget. In the middle of a large dining room four of us sat at a relatively small round table. Opposite me was a lady historian. Lord and Lady Rosebery kept up a lively conversation, occasionally squabbling as though the two strangers were members of the family. I found it hilarious. The other curiosity was a huge sideboard which seemed to occupy the whole of one wall. On it was every brand of bottled sauce and pickle and, in the centre, a gun carriage supporting a huge bottle, not of brandy, but of Old Grandad Kentucky Bourbon.

With the exception of sample bottles removed for viewing and tasting, the Mentmore wines were packed up and removed by a friendly wine merchant and stored in his cellars in Oxford.

The pre-sale tasting held under the front doorsteps of Christie's was, by present-day standards, unbelievable. It included: from Dalmeny and Mentmore bottles of Lafite of the 1858 and 1874 vintages, Latour 1874, Pichon circa 1870, Corton 1865, Sillery 1857 and 1874, Marcobrunner Auslese 1886, Schloss Johannisberger 1920, Milk Punch circa 1750 and 1830 (both from Hopetoun), and even a rare California wine – Sweet Muscatel from the Palo Alto Vineyard, Menlo Park, now a fashionable residential area near Stanford University.

The sale itself (I never need to look up the date or details) took place in the Great Rooms on Thursday 31st May, 1967. It was a milestone in the history of the Wine Department. Indeed, it put us on our feet. The catalogue attracted the attention and bids of connoisseurs and collectors all over the world.

It was to be the first of many sales of 'Finest and Rarest Wines'! The title page was bristling with titles: *The Properties of* The Most Honourable The MARQUESS OF LINLITHGOW, The Right Honourable The EARL OF ROSEBERY AND KINGHORN, KT, of Amiya, Dowager COUNTESS OF SANDWICH, The Right Honourable The LORD BRUNTISFIELD, a colonel, a major, and MRS WATNEY, the widow of a brewery magnate.

A brief summary of the contents of the sale follows: From Hopetoun House (Linlithgow), lots 129 to 195 – a magnum of 1740 Canary wine with

A relaxed Ian and Peter Symington.

Painting of Oporto by
Napier Henry (1881) owned
by John Delaforce.

Aerating a vat of
tawny port.

Opposite
Terracing at Quinta
do Noval.

Dawn in the Western Oregon vineyards,
(Willamette Valley appelation) with 11,500 foot Mount Hood in the background.

its original bin label, a dozen shapely mid-eighteenth century half bottles of Milk Punch, four bottles of the original and forbidden *extrait d'Absinthe* and other old liqueurs, no fewer than eight dozen bottles of Sandeman's 1911 Coronation vintage port – if you ever see a bottle of this rarity it will almost certainly have come from the Hopetoun cellars. There was also some decent claret, old burgundy, including Corton Grancey from the Café Voisin, the most fashionable restaurant in Paris around the mid-nineteenth century. An 1869 Hermitage, an 1868 Johannisberger Castle and old champagne.

Dalmeny overlooking the Firth of Forth.

All this was leading up to the Rosebery collection which comprised lots 196 to 313 in the same sale. It opened with three bottles of 1830 Tokay from Mentmore, and madeira of the same year which had been shipped from Madeira via Baltimore. Then, after nearly seven dozen pale dry sherry bottles about 1870, came the 'remarkable and extremely rare selection of the great pre-phylloxera wines of the "Golden Age" of Claret – 1858 to 1878': nineteen magnums and six bottles of the 1858 Lafite, a single magnum of the most renowned 1864, two 'triple-magnums' (jeroboams) of the deep coloured and long lasting 1865, forty-four magnums and five dozen and ten bottles of the 1874. Then Latour: twenty bottles of the 1874, and two magnums of Mouton 1878.

The rest of the collection, rich as it was, seemed an anti-climax: eighteen bottles of 1865 Corton, masses of old hock in perfect condition, from an

1862 Schloss Johannisberg to a 1921 Schloss Vollrads; Moselle, from an 1893 Wiltinger Kupp to a delightful 1933 Avelsbacher Herrenberg, Füder No. 195.

The wine which fascinated me, because it is so rarely seen, was the old Sillery, described by me in the catalogue as 'A still dry champagne of high quality, especially esteemed in Paris and in the better English houses throughout the XVIII and XIXth centuries'. Judging from its rare appearances in Christie catalogues of the last century, and the prices paid, it was a highly desirable, if strange, wine. The vintages of Sillery in the Rosebery cellars included the great 1857 and 1865, in magnums and bottles, 1871 and 1874 – the latter perhaps the most fabled and highest priced of all champagne vintages. Also of this vintage was Ay Crémant and Delamotte. It is hard to imagine what the Sillery was like in its prime. At roughly a century old it was still a palish, straw colour, the bouquet strange, nutty – not unlike a *vin de paille* from the Jura, and dry on the palate to the point of austerity. Something of an acquired taste, but a fascinating experience.

And the prices? They were extraordinary then. They look unbelievable bargains now. It is not just a question of world demand for such rarities having increased. After all it takes only two bidders to establish a price, and we had a lot of wealthy bidders in 1967. The main culprit is inflation. Everything has gone up umpteen times since then. So, frankly, it is pointless to list the prices.

Was the wine drunk? Most of it has been. One of the triple-magnums of 1865 Lafite was consumed (to my horror – I would have advised a longer rest) by Mark Birley and friends at Annabels only a week or so after the sale. It was superb. The second was shipped to California and, after being left for a year to settle, was the centrepiece of a notable black-tie dinner in San Francisco. It was decanted very ingeniously, by syphoning it into decanters – a trick I have used successfully since with other large bottles – and was superb, faultless.

Lord Rosebery said to me, 'I do not entertain as much as I used to. I am too old for big dinner parties, and to open a triple-magnum for sixteen or eighteen people, of whom only one or two would *really* appreciate its rarity and beauty would be a waste'. My reply was that I perfectly understood this and that a sale would be a marvellous opportunity to give a lot of other connoisseurs the opportunity to acquire wines which would otherwise simply be unobtainable. I was sure that his nectar would tantalise appreciative noses and caress appreciative palates. He agreed. And it did.

Opposite
Hopetoun House near
Edinburgh.

THE FIRST GROWTHS OF BORDEAUX

Their Evolution and Influence

Edmund Penning-Rowsell

Like God, as Voltaire put it, if the first growths of Bordeaux did not exist it would be necessary to invent them. For from their inception roughly three centuries ago they have contributed so much to the glory and reputation of Bordeaux in general and of claret in particular that it is difficult to imagine the world of wine without them. Although not necessarily always the finest wines of their vintage, the original four – for Mouton-Rothschild, Ausone, Cheval-Blanc and Pétrus must be considered in a later historical context – formed a collective touchstone of quality by which fine claret has in general been judged. And without proclaimed first growths would there have been second, third, fourth or fifth growths? Indeed would there have been a classification at all, narrow as it is? Pomerol, admittedly a comparative newcomer on the Bordeaux scene, has got along very well without one.

Moreover, we British played a great part in their continued existence and, indirectly at least, in their classification. Initially their existence and success depended on the support of the English – and no doubt Scottish, Welsh and Irish – nobility and later of the prosperous new middle classes. There may exist somewhere in French archives references similar to those of Samuel Pepys, who in 1663 recorded that he 'drank a sort of French wine called Ho Bryan that hath a good and most particular taste that I never met with', or around forty years later, to announcements in the official *London Gazette* of a sale of 'Lafit, Margouze and La Tour', but if so they have never come to light. Good wine needs good, regular customers and consumers, and these originally lay principally in England, thanks, curiously enough, to the Anglo-French wars at the beginning of the eighteenth century. For these sale announcements were of wines taken from captured French ships, although where the precious cargoes were intended for remains a mystery; possibly the Netherlands, but their economic power was by then on the wane, and what they bought in Bordeaux, and presumably shipped

Château Haut-Brion

in their own ships, was chiefly inexpensive wines, mostly white.

It is an interesting sidelight on the demand for this new, expensive claret, that these captured wines arrived soon after the Methuen Treaty with Portugal in 1703 imposed a duty on French wines – and later too on Spanish wines – fifty per cent higher than that on Portuguese. Whether these original landings, auctioned in coffee-houses in the City of London, paid duty is not clear, but certainly the later ones did. They were heavy, but clearly the wealthy British consumers shrugged them off.

However, if on this side of the English Channel there was a new, rich clientele for fine claret, its production and improvement were only possible because on the other side a new rich class had arisen – the *noblesse de robe*, mostly lawyers some of whom had salted away part of their fees into property, including vineyard land. One may assume that the Haut-Brion that Pepys drank was from a reasonably mature vineyard, established perhaps about 1650, but the other leading vineyards were almost certainly planted in the 1670s or early 1680s. Latour was bought by a rich man whose great-niece, Marie-Thérèse de Clauzel, inherited it in 1693 and who, two years later, married Alexandre de Ségur, who already owned Lafite, as well

Château Ausone

CHATEAU AUSONE
PREMIER GRAND CRU CLASSÉ DE SAINT-ÉMILION
Madame DUBOIS-CHALLON & Héritiers C. VAUTHIER, Propriétaires

At Château Latour

as what later was to become Brane-Mouton. Margaux was owned by the Marquis d'Aulède, who also had a half-share of Haut-Brion. These were very rich families, particularly in the next generation, who were able to develop their properties. The vineyard of Lafite was doubled between 1680 and 1750. Jacques de Ségur's son, the Marquis Nicolas Alexandre de Ségur, was known as *'le Prince des Vignes'*, and when he died in 1755 he was the richest man in Bordeaux, then at the peak of its prosperity. The Pontac family, principal proprietors of Haut-Brion, owned the grandest house in the Bordeaux, the Maison Daurade.

Nevertheless, while such men could develop their vineyards and have good wine made, they could not sell it themselves: there were no cellar-door sales at Château Lafite. Fortunately, however, this gap between producer and overseas consumer was soon made good by newcomers from the British Isles: merchants who had emigrated to Bordeaux principally from Scotland and Ireland, with the main purpose of trading with their native lands. The best-known today are the Bartons and the Johnstons, but they were not the first. These merchants had almost a monopoly of the wine trade with Britain, and this enabled them to maintain the upper hand in dealing even with the first growths, an ascendancy largely maintained until after the Second World War. For a good two centuries an annual contest took place between the Bordeaux brokers acting on behalf of the merchants and the managers (*régisseurs*) of the first growths as to the prices of the new wines. These prices were of vital concern to the former, for at least until the middle of the last century there was a well-established 'staircase' for the other classed growths, with the fifth paid ex-cellars at half the price of the firsts. So the more these were squeezed the less would be paid for the rest. Incidentally, prices remained stable from about 1725 for a century and more, in a way almost incredible in the light of today's inflation-ridden trade. In a good year the first growths might then expect to secure 2,000 francs a *tonneau* for their wine.

The establishment of a classification (almost entirely of the Médoc alone) was the work of the Bordeaux brokers and appears to have existed unofficially by 1730 when, in a report quoted by André Simon in *Bottlescrew Days* (1926), three principal classes of red wine were recorded. 'The first comprises the growths of Pontac (Haut-Brion), Lafitte and Château de Margo, which produce as a rule only about three hundred tuns a year; this is, however, the wine most highly esteemed of the province ... It is the English who buy the greater part of this wine.' Perhaps Latour was not mentioned because it was then part of the Ségur estate, and only became independent in 1760 when it passed into the hands of three of the Marquis Alexandre's daughters and their husbands. When Thomas Jefferson visited Bordeaux in 1787 he included 'La Tour de Ségur' among the 'the four vineyards of first quality', and he also mentioned a small number of seconds and thirds.

Further unofficial classifications were reported during the eighteenth century, based more on communes than on individual growths, with Pauillacs and Margaux fetching more than St Juliens and Cantenacs. By the end of the century the three classes were extended to four and then, about 1820, to five.

There is no doubt, however, that for a very long time the first growths dominated the English market, and until near the end of the eighteenth century their individual names were not of prime importance, as can be seen from the sale catalogues of Christie's, which sold wine from the firm's foundation in 1766. In July 1787 ten hogsheads 'of High flavour'd Claret of the first growths' were offered at £34.00 a hogshead, and bottles at 36s a dozen. The following year the château names are mentioned for the first time: Lafete (sic) and Château Margeaux (sic) that sold for 66s and 49s a dozen respectively. Yet plain 'St Julian' fetched 60s at the same sale. All wines were, of course, imported in cask. In 1797 six hogsheads of '1st growth Claret of 1791 considered the best that France has produced for many years, and similar is difficult at this time to be obtained, and now in high order for bottling'. They went for 56/57 guineas apiece. The lateness of

the bottling may be noted, and until about 1830-1840 four-year bottlings were the rule, owing perhaps to an excess of tannin in wine made from grapes picked early to lessen the risks of poor autumn weather.

An old engraving of Château Mouton-Rothschild.

For well over a century Lafite was certainly the most esteemed first growth, as claimed in the sale notice of 1797 when the state-confiscated château was sold. In the first edition of Cocks et Féret's *Bordeaux et ses Vins* (1850) Lafite is given as having for several years sold at the highest price and 'almost all is consumed in England'. Later still, this primacy was confirmed in the series of splendid country mansion cellars the contents of which were unearthed and sold by Christie's from 1967 onwards. In almost all, the leading wines were Lafites. And, whether or not justified by quality, who can deny that this still applies to a large extent today? Excluding Pétrus, whose prices at auction reflect its small output as much as its quality, Lafite, after its opening price, nearly always commands the highest figure.

It is clear from Christie's records that it was a very long time before even the second growths acquired much individual acclaim. Apart from the firsts, claret was either sold with a commune name or, from the beginning of the nineteenth century, under the name of the merchants who had imported and bottled it – nearly all located in the region of St James's. The first mention in a Christie catalogue of a second growth was in 1829 when Léoville 1820, shipped by Barton & Guestier, was sold for 66s a dozen.

Château Mouton-
Rothschild

Larose (Gruaud-Larose) appeared next in 1834, and only in April of that
year was Mouton first listed and selling for 42s a dozen; albeit the same
price as Lafite and Latour. Rauzan was catalogued first in 1845 and Cos
d'Estournel in 1848. But for many years the two seconds most prominent
in the auction rooms were Léoville and (Gruaud-) Larose.

Up to the Revolution the first growths seemed to have been very
profitable, but for a long time afterwards they experienced a series of
difficulties, of which the oidium fungus attack, from 1852 to 1857, was the
worst. But this was followed by the most prosperous period Bordeaux was
to know until the last fifteen years. At a time when great fortunes were
being made by entrepreneurs of many kinds to whom the label on the
bottle at their extravagant tables was probably the most important feature,
the first growths sold for very high prices.

This period ended abruptly with the phylloxera, which struck the Médoc in force in 1880, and the mildew a few years later. Output declined sharply and, to counteract this, the first-growth and other properties over-manured their vineyards, leading to a big drop in quality and reputation. Claret was 'out' in favour of champagne, and only partially regained its position after the last world war although, of course, it retained its dedicated admirers.

The 'campaign' to promote Mouton to a first growth appears to have started before its acquisition by the Rothschild family in 1853. Originally a part of the Lafite estate, it was planted before 1725, probably by Joseph de Brane. In the middle of that century its wines fetched prices on a level with those of the second growths, and although by the time of the official classification in 1855 it was acknowledged to be 'the first of the seconds' its prices were still lower than those of the firsts. This indeed was why it was made a second growth, for the classification of the Bordeaux brokers was based on the levels of price over a long period; and although in the 1860s voices were to be heard declaring that Mouton-Rothschild should be a first growth, in that booming period its prices were markedly below those of its rivals. Between then and the arrival of the young Baron Philippe in 1922, the family took little direct interest in the estate, which was run by managers. But Baron Philippe changed all that, although his relentless fight

Château Cheval-Blanc

Château Pétrus

to become a first growth only developed after the Second World War and finally achieved success in 1973; certainly with justification.

The other three generally acknowledged first growths, Ausone, Cheval-Blanc and Pétrus, came on the scene much later. It has been said that Ausone was omitted from the 1855 classification because of its tiny area (seven hectares) but, although listed among forty-two St Emilions in the 1853 edition of Wilhelm Franck's *Traité sur les Vins du Médoc et les Autres*, it is not singled out for any special mention, while Cheval-Blanc is listed among the seconds. The failure of Ausone to make outstanding wine over many years, as well as an apparent lack of ambition on the part of its owners, led to its public neglect; however, this has changed in the last ten years, and its opening prices are at least equal to those of the other first growths and, on account of its small output, often higher.

Cheval-Blanc, carved out of the Figeac estate in 1834, first achieved some prominence in 1862 when it won a bronze medal, still reproduced on its label, at the London International Exhibition of that year. But its international reputation was achieved with its famous 1921, a fabulously rich, port-like wine. This was followed by other outstanding vintages capped, in the post-war era, by the 1947. In reputation and price it is now firmly fixed among the first growths.

Pétrus really only came to the fore after World War II, notably with its 1947; however, its special qualities of richness and concentration of bouquet and flavour were not really appreciated until the sixties, when the American market for fine claret first developed on a large scale. Now its quality, combined with small production – about forty *tonneaux* compared with 200 or more for the Médoc *premiers* – has placed it *hors concours* among its peers, although it is careful to maintain its opening prices on a level with theirs. However, since no prestigious American cellar is complete without an array of Pétrus, its price on the market and in the auction room is much higher than theirs; this is partly too for speculation/investment purposes.

This investment/speculation factor has affected Bordeaux on a

Château Lafite

Château Latour

considerable scale since the end of the sixties and has reflected widespread attempts to find hedges against the inflation whose fluctuations have dominated much financial thinking ever since. Also, from the fifties onwards, first growth prices began to rise out of relation to the seconds, influenced to some extent by the Mouton-Rothschild/Lafite rivalry in which both estates endeavoured to offer their wines initially at higher prices than the other. The start of the London wine auctions – Christie's in 1966 and Sotheby's in 1970 – also stimulated the investment/speculation boom, which temporarily came to a disastrous end in 1973/74, and forced Latour, Lafite and Mouton-Rothschild to sell their wines at Christie's.

Not unnaturally, the second growths and those like Palmer, Beychevelle and Lynch-Bages of a similar status, felt that in comparison with the first growths and the high prices that their own wines later fetched at auction, they were under-valuing these. So they too have been offered *en primeur* at ever higher prices, which may attract investors but put them out of reach of many serious amateurs of fine claret. Moreover the financial inability of the trade, in Bordeaux and elsewhere, any longer to hold much stock has meant that the latest vintage, if generally acceptable, is passed on as quickly as possible to the retail customer, whether drinker or investor; and the wines have to be bought at least by the single case, which many drinkers

Château Margaux

can neither afford nor later accommodate. Moreover, unless and until there is another slump this has to be the most economical way of buying popular classed growths, especially the firsts.

In my view at least, these developments, if to some extent inevitable in the world in which we live, are unfortunate for Bordeaux. If the American market now partly occupies the position that the British once did nearly three centuries ago, the latter is still vitally important for the classed growths, and possibly less volatile than the former. Unfortunately there has grown up a view in Bordeaux that if a château offers its wine at a lower price than its neighbour, it must be less good. This nonsense should be cut out. While at present the first growths seem caught in an irreversible price spiral, the other echelons of the classed growths might well appreciate that much of the extra revenue received, from prices little connected with their production costs falls into the hands of the tax collector, and that for their reputations to be maintained their wines must be drunk. This applies to the first growths too, which for so long have been the standard bearers of Bordeaux throughout the wine-drinking world.

FOOD FIT FOR A QUEEN

Serena Sutcliffe

A long time ago, I heard something about this royal lunch. The venerable owner of Baumanière, M Raymond Thuilier, had discreetly let it slip that the Queen had had his establishment recommended to her by the Queen Mother, already a devotee of the place! And the Queen Mother's gastronomic advice is to be followed, for there is no one in the Royal Family more interested and knowledgeable on the subject.

All the jewels of Provence were laid out for the Monarch. Sea bass, the *loup de mer* of the south, is the most regal fish in the repertory – here *farci* (what with, one wonders – fennel, or perhaps shrimps?) *et en croûte*. Chevalier-Montrachet Les Demoiselles 1964 would have been rich and powerful enough to pay court to the fleshy *loup*.

Her Majesty arrives for lunch on 17 May 1972.

EN L'OUSTAU DE BAUMANIÈRE

Loup farci en croûte sauce crevettes

Gigot d'agneau au poivre vert

Petits pois frais du jardin

Mousseline d'artichauts

Plateau de fromages

Sorbet au citron

Fraises à la crème

Millefeuilles

Friandises Baumanière

CHEVALIER-MONTRACHET "LES DEMOISELLES" 1964

CHATEAU MARGAUX 1955

PIPER HEIDSIECK CUVÉE FLORENS LOUIS 1964

L'Oustau de Baumanière
at Les Baux.

This meant that the main course could not be one of Baumanière's lasting
specialities, *gigot d'agneau en croûte* – two sets of pastry would have defeated
most of us, let alone the Queen's known delicate appetite. So, here, the
gigot was served *au poivre vert*, another reminder of the Mediterranean, with
petits pois which most certainly did not come out of a tin and a *mousseline
d'artichauts* which must have been delicious (and artichokes go wonderfully
with wine). Only a first growth would do on this occasion, and it was
Margaux 1955, not one of the greatest years for this *château* – but 1972 was
the right time to drink it for its comparatively youthful charm and fruit.

Obviously, the luncheon party would have kept right on sipping the
Margaux over the *plateau de fromages* which, one hopes, would have
included some tempting provençal *barons*, all done up in their chestnut
leaves.

I certainly would not have sipped my Cuvée Florens Louis 1964 with my
sorbet au citron, as that is cruelty to champagne. It is a truly French tradition
to serve Brut champagne with *le dessert*, but it would have been no hardship
at all to let it slip down with *fraises à la crème* and those famous Baumanière
millefeuilles. Whether I would have reached the *friandises* is a moot point, but
perhaps Her Majesty was allowed to take some away in a box. Ah, *la belle
France cossue* . . .

STRENGTH THROUGH RESIN

Patrick Leigh Fermor

The wine that washed down this late and long drawn-out second breakfast seemed to attach wings to our heels. We flew along the side of the rocky coast at mercurial speed, in spite of the sun's ascent.

There is a lot to be said for starting the day like this. In dashing households in many mountain villages the day begins with a minute cup of Turkish coffee, a doorstep of black bread, a handful of olives, hunks of rank and excellent goat's cheese, and a glass – or several glasses – of fiery distilled spirits. In Epirus, northern Thessaly and Macedonia, slugs of bracing *tsipouro* often usher in the day and in Crete, where the practice is more widespread, down, each at a single swashbuckling gulp, go several glasses of *tsikoudia,* the Cretan raki distilled from the stalks, skins and pips after the grape-treading, sometimes deliciously flavoured with crushed mulberries. Each shot drops to its destination with the smoothness of a tracer-bullet and the somnolent organism is roused with the same shock as that of an oyster under the lemon, summoning startled gasps from the novice and making his eyes leap from their sockets. 'One more', says the flask-wielding host, 'just to kill the microbe. *Dia na skotosome to mikrovio.'* And so the gnawing worm of death's sister, sleep, is scotched anew each morning and up one starts ready to tackle whatever the day may bring with the optimism, the vigour and the dauntlessness of a giant. There is a great deal of ritual drinking-terminology and singing and inter-weaving of toasts in Greece, and it is in Crete that they reach their most elaborate flowering. Often it is an antiphony of challenge and response. 'May we become as rich as the Sultan Amurath! – *Sta Mourátia mas!'* they cry in some villages on Mount Kedros, and 'May the All-Holy One scour the rust from our guns.' It is only there that one hears, with great astonishment, on the morning after a long dionysiac vigil, an exact echo of a certain well-known English phrase: 'Of the dog that has bitten you', they say, 'throw in some of the fur.' *'Skýli pou se dángose, vále ap' to malí tou.'* And then comes the soft *glou-glou* of pouring fur . . .

There is a tendency to drink in unison after a concentric clink of glasses, a solitary drinker usually giving a ritual tap to the glasses standing nearest. How often have I heard this clinking explained: how the fifth sense of hearing, not only taste, sight, smell and touch, must be requited! Then, purely for fun, there is drinking *kalogerí stika* – monkishly: grasping the little tumblers in the palm of their hands the drinkers muffle the impact of glass on glass by only touching knuckles ('so that the abbot won't hear us'). Not that there is any need of secrecy in Greek monasteries. Many of them are famous not only for their vineyards and their lavish hospitality, but for the jovial and Friar Tuck-ish capacities of the brethren. There is a rare and charming Cretan custom of drinking 'like little frogs' – *ta vatrachákia*, it is called or, on the deeper dialect, *t'aphordakákia*. Two drinkers hold their glasses lightly by the upper rim furthest from them, and swing them gently together so that the bottom edges intershock, bounce away and strike again with a series of light impacts that mimic a soft and far-away croaking. It is repeated thrice. *'Vrekekekex!'* murmurs one. *'Koax!'* the other; and at the third time both murmur a final *'Koax!'* in unison. Wine glasses are never filled more than half, on the principle that one drinks more that way; it goes down in one gulp and needs restocking at once.

Some of the old 'black' and amber-coloured wines of Crete are followed next day by an aftermath which is only to be allayed by a glass or two of the same fur and the delicious frothing egg-and-lemon soup which is the pan-Hellenic nostrum for hangovers.

Retsina, however, tipped into the little tumblers from carafes, or better still, from chipped blue enamel mugs which are replenished again and again from vast barrels, seems to possess the secret of inducing high spirits and rash and uninhibited conduct with no sad retribution, as though a plenary absolution accompanied every gulp. This, for those lucky enough to like it as I do, places retsina high on the list of the manifold charms of Greece. Nobody seems to know when the Gods first treated their wine with resin. Certainly it was known in byzantine days. Some place its origin much further back, basing their assumption on the pine-cone, which, in old sculptures, sometimes tops the vinewreathed thyrsus of Dionysius. It is assumed that the taste began fortuiously with the custom of caulking the leaks in barrels and wine skins with lumps of resin. The vine- and pine-clad slopes of Attica are its true habitat, but many other regions are famous. Perhaps the two most celebrated sources, both for drinking on the spot and for export to regions and islands less generously blessed, are the ancient town of Megara, half-way between Athens and Corinth, and Karystos in Euboea. Bad retsina can be extruciatingly nasty; the best – and Athenian tavernas, except for a few which remain unswervingly reliable, show an alarming tendency to degenerate in this matter – is incomparably good. It should never, to my mind, be drunk outside Greece, for one of its secrets is drinking it with unstinted abundance. It seems to have an alliance with the air in the promotion of well-being. Many people think that it bestows the gift of bodily health as well; a belief I accept at once without further scrutiny.

MARCHESI ANTINORI: NEW TRADITIONS AFTER 600 YEARS

Burton Anderson

Italian vintners still speak reverently of their millennial heritage of wines and vines, even though radical change over the last two decades seems to have turned the term 'tradition' into a fatally overworked cliché.

Contrasts between reality and myth were dramatised in 1985 when the house which has most influenced Italy's revolution in viniculture, Marchesi L & P Antinori of Florence, celebrated its 600th anniversary. Though not oblivious to the event's potential ironies, Piero Antinori, current head of the family firm, focused on actualities during the year-long festivities, admirably avoiding easy lapses into platitudes.

'It does seem exceptional for a family to have 600 years of experience in any field, especially wine', he said that autumn, during a rare break in his schedule. 'The anniversary gave us a chance to pause and look back a moment and weigh the very real responsibilities of having such a history. But we don't feel burdened by the past. On the contrary, we used the sixth centenary theme to emphasise our role as innovators, to call attention to our present activities and the future – to what I like to call our new traditions.'

From a multiple base of estates and cellars in Tuscany and neighbouring Umbria, Marchesi Antinori have moved boldly but astutely to revise the styles of such classics as chianti and Orvieto while creating 'new traditions' with such wines as Tignanello and Solaia. Other wineries, large and small, have followed suit, creating new-wave wines with such intensity that the movement has been referred to as a renaissance. The aspiring masters are many, but if one individual deserves to be singled out as prime mover of the modern *rinascimento* it is Piero Antinori.

When Piero took over from his father, Niccolò, in the late 1960s, Antinori was a leading name in chianti. Today it is pre-eminent not only in Tuscany but in all of Italy. Marchesi L & P Antinori, more emphatically than any

SECENTENARIO
ANTINORI

[handwritten archival text]

Il giorno 19 del mese di maggio 1385
Giovanni di Piero Antinori, quartiere di Santo Spirito, popolo di San Iacopo, gonfalone del Nicchio, vinattiere novizio, personalmente ecc., giurò ecc., promise ecc., si impegnò ecc., rinunciò ecc., al fine ecc., essendo garante Giandonato vinattiere...

FIRENZE, ARCHIVIO DI STATO, ARTE DEI VINATTIERI (FOGLIO C 30 RECTO)

Specimen

Imbottigliato da Marchesi L. e P. Antinori in occasione del seicentenario enoico della famiglia Antinori, in San Casciano V.P. - 382 Firenze - Italia

1500 ml. ℮ - 12,5% vol. VINO DA TAVOLA

ANTINORI 1385-1985 **600** ANNIVERSARIO

other large-scale winery, projects an image of historical class that gives a certain aura even to its everyday wines.

Among the Florentine houses, it is neither the oldest (Marchesi de' Frescobaldi traces its origins to 1308) nor the most legendary (Brolio with the 'Iron Baron' Bettino Ricasoli probably qualifies as that). Antinori's singular status is rather a recent phenomenon attributable to good sense, good taste and good fortune, a combination which when totalled up seems magically greater than the sum of its parts. And though Piero Antinori has authored what may be the most exciting chapter in the firm's six hundred-year history, before putting the spotlight on contemporary feats, it seems only fitting to dwell for a bit in the past.

The founding has a precise date: 19 May, 1385, when Giovanni di Piero Antinori registered as an apprentice in the newly formed guild known as *Arte dei Vinattieri*. In that era, the making and selling of wine was still a secondary line of work in Florence, whose prominent citizens were building fortunes in the silk and wool trades and banking. The Antinori

Above Reproduced on the label is Giovanni di Piero Antinori's registration into the *Arte dei Vinattieri*, found in the Florentine state archive in the 1385 register.

Opposite Piero Antinori (right) with father Niccolò and brother, Ludovico, at the 600th anniversary celebrations in Florence.

family was no exception; Giovanni's relatives may well have viewed his debut as a vintner with a jaundiced eye.

Yet the Antinori link with wine endured long after silk and banking activities waned. Giovanni's son and grandson were enrolled in the same guild in the fifteenth century. Though little was recorded about them, they must have done well, for work began on the splendid Palazzo Antinori, on what was to become the Piazza degli Antinori in the heart of Florence, and the family also acquired choice property on the outskirts of town.

Charles V's troops occupied the land during the siege of Florence in 1530. A decade later, the Emperor's fleet seized a cargo of Malvasia wine belonging to Antinori off Messina in Sicily and used it to refresh the troops. Though reimbursement was promised, three years later Senator Alessandro Antinori implored Tuscany's Duke Cosimo de' Medici to speak to Charles V about arranging for 'just payment' of the debt.

The wines of Antinori won an endorsement in the seventeenth century when the poet-physician Francesco Redi lauded one in his epic poem *Bacco in Toscana*. An approximately literal translation follows:

'There at Antinoro up in those haughty hills,
That have taken the name of the Roses,
Oh what joy, oh how
From the blackest grapes
Of a ripe Canaiolo
I squeeze a must so pure,
That in glasses (it) gushes,
Leaps, sparkles and gleams!'

The Antinori, like other aristocratic Florentine families, expanded their agricultural holdings during the eighteenth and nineteenth centuries, making and selling wine and olive oil along with other produce. Previously, Tuscany had been noted as much for its white and sweet wines as for dry reds. But chianti was becoming more prominent, thanks to the works of such men as Bettino Ricasoli, who composed a formula for production, and to Laborel Melini, who devised a flask strong enough to be sealed with a cork for shipping the wine throughout the world.

In 1873, Niccolò Antinori won a Diploma of Distinction for his wines at the World Exposition of Vienna. And though he considered commercialising the products of the family's four farms under a single trademark, it was not until 1898 that his sons Lodovico and Piero formed the actual wine company known as Marchesi L & P Antinori. They built the cellars at San Casciano Val di Pesa, where the main vinification plant is today, and began to export to other European countries and America.

The Antinori product line ranged beyond chianti (which was then also a white wine – an historical privilege summarily removed by *denominazione di origine controllata*) to include a sweet red Aleatico and a sparkling Gran Spumante Marchese Antinori. To make the latter, the brothers Antinori hired a cellarmaster from Rheims and equipped their *cantine* with *pupitres* and other paraphernalia for the *méthode champenoise*. It was convincing enough for the composer, Giacomo Puccini, in a letter to Piero Antinori in 1914, to compare it to Mumm's Cordon Rouge, then the *ne plus ultra* of champagne.

Piero's son Niccolò moved into the company in the mid-1920s and is still there, even though he delegated the management to his sons Piero and

Opposite
The Castello della Sala near Orvieto on the borders of Umbria and Tuscany. It was built in the fourteenth century.

A fresco in the Castello della Sala.

Lodovico in 1965 and now dedicates much of his time to writing, reading and an almost daily round of golf. It was Niccolò who weathered depression and war and the almost disastrous demise of chianti into the peninsula's most widely imitated plonk and, through his unrelenting insistence on quality, carried the Antinori name to new levels of respect.

He also set the stage for further success with his acquisitions of Santa Cristina (including Tignanello) in Chianti Classico, Castello della Sala in Orvieto and the Tenuta dei Della Gherardesca at Bolgheri on the Tuscan coast. At one point, to raise funds to keep Palazzo Antinori in the family, he was forced to sell the estate of San Martino alla Palma. With that he lost the model for the villa depicted on the Villa Antinori label, but since the place was bombarded in the Second World War and modified in reconstruction, it no longer looked the same anyway.

Niccolò Antinori, who typically credits his accomplishments to his able collaborators, likes the eulogy conferred on him by the former mayor of Florence, Piero Bargellini, as a man who 'between the jesting and the serious, to the title of *marchese* preferred that of vintner.'

With semi-retirement, his oldest son, Piero ('the serious-minded one') took charge. Lodovico (the 'fun-loving one') oversees the markets for olive oil and is developing another estate at Bolgheri.

Piero Antinori, who had studied economics and commerce in Italy and abroad, had also done a *stage* in Bordeaux with family friend and adviser, Emile Peynaud. But he quickly recognised that his role in the firm was as administrator, leaving the technical aspects of wine making to oenologist Giacomo Tachis.

One of Piero's first moves was to convince his uncle, Mario Incisa della Rocchetta, to bottle the Cabernet he had been making at Bolgheri and market it through Antinori. Incisa, heeding tips from Tachis and Peynaud, perhaps uniquely in Italy, aged his wine in small French barrels. It worked. Sassicaia from 1972 went on to win a *Decanter* tasting in 1978 as the best of thirty-four Cabernets from eleven countries and become the legend that Hugh Johnson still refers to as 'perhaps Italy's best red wine'.

Then came Tignanello, created by Antinori and Tachis in 1971 as a single vineyard wine from Santa Cristina, based on *sangiovese* and aged in *barriques*, but then with a hint of *canaiolo* and white *malvasia* in the blend. In 1975, it took on *cabernet* and lost the *canaiolo* and *malvasia*. Though no longer strictly speaking a *cru*, it has the distinction of being Italy's most imitated red wine. Beyond that, it had become the Antinori symbol of what chianti might be.

Antinori and Tachis have campaigned for the elimination of white grapes from chianti, while favouring *cabernet* as the complement to *sangiovese*, which would give the wine better colour, bouquet and that hitherto evasive flavour quality known as *souplesse*. They claimed a victory in 1984 when chianti became DOCG (government guaranteed) and the new formula for Classico cut the white grapes to two per cent minimum (tantamount to none at all) and approved *cabernet, merlot* and *pinot noir* as complementary varieties.

Rather than showing complacency over the triumphs, Antinori has been stepping up the pace. The two most recent releases have a decidedly 'international' tone. Solaia is a single-vineyard Cabernet from Santa Cristina that drew immediate comparisons to Sassicaia and California Cabernets. Secentenario, issued in 26,000 magnums to celebrate the anniversary, is a masterful blend of *merlot* and *cabernet*.

More novelties are awaited, as experimental plantings of *chardonnay, sauvignon-blanc*, the *pinots* and *aleatico* at Castello della Sala, reach maturity. Cellars there have been completely refurbished to handle the series of *crus*. Antinori also recently purchased Villa Terciona to augment its holdings in Chianti Classico.

'We're carrying out intensive research into wine making techniques', said Piero Antinori, 'though with Tachis in charge, oenology is our strongpoint.

The glorious rolling hills of Italy with their cypresses, vines, olives and flowers.

Our most demanding work now is in the vineyards. There is still so much to learn there in terms of selection of clones and rootstocks, plant density, training methods and proper yields for our special conditions of climate and terrain. We've needed to change the philosophy behind grape growing, turning the obsession with quantity into a quest for quality.'

He was talking in his office in the Palazzo Antinori, where he lives with his wife, Francesca, a Roman princess, and his three daughters. Trim and vital, Piero Antinori seems younger than forty-eight, a modern *marchese* who lives up to the description of dashing more in appearance than manner. Though he moves with aristocratic ease, dresses impeccably and can converse unaffectedly in several languages, like his father he has a modest air about him that gives his words down-to-earth sincerity.

He travels abroad frequently ('too frequently', as he lamented on one brilliant autumn morning toward the end of the 600th year) and tastes others' wines with an open and searching mind. It was characteristic of the man, who likes to mention that his mother's great-grandfather was American, to serve wines from France, Spain and California along with his own at the centenary banquet in May. To celebrate the event, he also gave dinners and tastings in the United Kingdom, the United States, Ireland, Canada, Holland, Switzerland, West Germany and France and was planning a visit to Japan in the near future.

Unlike so many of his Tuscan colleagues, Piero Antinori is not convinced that the world's best wines are now being made in Tuscany, though he seems to have little doubt that some of them soon will be.

'We have exceptional natural conditions here in certain places, and a variety of microclimates going from quite warm to quite cool', he said. 'But we have only begun to do what the French did long ago, to co-ordinate our vine varieties with their ideal habitat. You know, it seems hard to believe that after six hundred years we still have so much to accomplish. In a sense, Italy is a young wine country with so much potential and so many challenges to meeting it. But that's what makes this work so fascinating.'

Perhaps to emphasise his accent on the future, he asked his daughter Albiera to join us. At eighteen, she is already working part time in the business and would soon be off for a *stage* in the United States.

'We've learned a lot about techniques from the French, of course, and also from California', he said. 'But I think we've reached a point now where it's essential that we develop along our own lines, create our own Italian styles. Whether we work with native Italian varieties, such as *sangiovese*, or with vines of foreign origin such as *cabernet* and *chardonnay*, our aim is to create wines with their own distinctive personalities. That's one reason why we never issue a wine with a varietal name. We want the wine to be considered on its own merits and not in relation to others of its species.'

He mentioned that experiments at Castello della Sala had indicated that *sauvignon-blanc* might benefit from blending with the local *grechetto*, just as *sauvignon* is often blended with *sémillon* in Bordeaux, or as *sangiovese* is blended with *cabernet* in Tignanello. He cited other projects underway in his vineyards and cellars but soon realised that there was not time enough to give all the details and his face broke into a grin, not devoid of exasperation.

'You know the difference between us and the French?', he mused. 'We have more fun. They've come close to reaching their peak. We haven't. We're not number one so we have to try harder. I like that challenge. It's inspiring, and I think it could become a distinct advantage for us in the future?'

He smiled again, but this time hope had erased exasperation. It was clear that by the future Piero Antinori was not referring to another 600 years.

MÜLLER-THURGAU AND SCHEU*

Helmut Becker

Professor Doctor Hermann Müller-Thurgau created the grape variety which bears his name in 1882 at Geisenheim in the Rheingau, by cross-breeding the *riesling* and *silvaner* vines, thus successfully initiating modern scientific cross-breeding of grape varieties. In 1891, Müller-Thurgau went to Switzerland to organise the creation of a research centre on the Geisenheim model in Wädenswil. Here he transferred 150 of his pre-tested seedlings, from which H Schellenberg selected the best, No 58, *riesling* x *silvaner*, and developed it.

In 1913, August Dern took cuttings of this new variety to Germany, naming it *müller-thurgau* in honour of the man who originally created it. The new type was subsequently introduced into many wine-growing countries, especially in Europe and New Zealand, where it is the most widely cultivated variety. Today the *müller-thurgau* grape covers about 24,000 hectares in the German Federal Republic, most German white wines being made from it. All in all, the total vineyard area covered by *müller-thurgau* the world over may well be in excess of 50,000 hectares.

Viticultural and oenological science reɡard Professor Müller-Thurgau as the founder of many different disciplines: he was the first botanist to concern himself specifically with the vine; he was the first to select species of wine yeast; he studied the physiology of fermentation, and was a phytopathologist as well as a breeder of grape varieties. All Geisenheim

(The quality and style of wine is due to several factors of which the grape itself is of course crucial. Good wine can only be made from good grapes and the latter depend on appropriate soil and climatic conditions, plus the skills of the grower and wine maker. The riesling *is the principal 'noble' vine variety in Germany but it is slow ripening in the colder northern latitudes like the Rheingau. The other much planted variety,* silvaner, *lacks the breed and bouquet of the* riesling. *In the late nineteenth century work began to produce vine strains which would override these problems and produce the perfect compromise. This chapter is about two of the pioneers. Editor.)*

A photograph of Professor Doctor Müller-Thurgau in 1882.

researchers are proud that in the work of Müller-Thurgau modern viticultural science had its beginning in Geisenheim. How many times a day do vintners and cellarers all over the world pronounce this name in the course of their work? And what about the countless wine enthusiasts who order a glass of Müller-Thurgau day by day and drink it with relish? No statistics tell us about them.

In considering the dissemination of this grape variety, we must also look at its origin, because that was an important factor in its naming. Twenty years ago the question of the variety's name was still a serious problem in German viticulture. Doubts had been raised as to whether it really was a *riesling* x *silvaner*; even the fact that Müller-Thurgau was the originator of the variety was being questioned and scientific opinion queried the *silvaner* 'paternity'.

It was now up to viticulturists at Geisenheim to clarify the case and defend Professor Müller-Thurgau. Our position was straightforward and unambiguous: there is absolutely no doubt that Müller-Thurgau is the originator of the variety. The name 'Müller-Thurgau' was already being used for the species in 1913 and had been published as such by his former assistant and colleague at Geisenheim, the Bavarian regional inspector for viticulture, August Dern. According to international law, objections to the name 'Müller-Thurgau' on grounds of misuse should have been raised before the lapse of fifty years. This had not happened; on the contrary in the beginning even Baden, together with all the other German regions and other wine-growing nations, had used the name 'Müller-Thurgau'.

Incidentally, Müller-Thurgau was this actual name: he was not Müller of the canton of Thurgau nor, as I read in one book, was Thurgau his wife's maiden name!

So, when the dispute was settled, *müller-thurgau* became the officially

Geisenheim in 1883. In one of the greenhouses the seedlings of the Müller-Thurgau crossing were raised.

sanctioned name for the grape variety. Today German wine lovers appreciate both the wine as well as its name, and most other European and overseas countries except Luxembourg and Switzerland also use the name *müller-thurgau*. Luxembourg calls it *rivaner*; New Zealand is in the process of making up its mind. Wine labels there bear the name 'Müller-Thurgau' as well as 'Riesling x Silvaner'. Switzerland is bound by tradition to keep to *'riesling x silvaner'*, the name in use in the days of Professor Müller-Thurgau, and the neighbouring countries respect this. In Germany there was an added reason for naming the variety *müller-thurgau*: according to German law no variety may be called after its parents; other *riesling* x *silvaner* cross-breeds are now in existence which have a different genetic constitution and must therefore not be mistaken for or compared with the *müller-thurgau riesling* x *silvaner*; *ehrenfelser*, for instance, or *osteiner*; *rieslaner* and *scheurebe* (the last two are recriprocal cross-breeds – *silvaner* x *riesling*).

The discussion over the origin of the *müller-thurgau* variety has had such a long-lasting effect that today even wine lovers who have no connection whatsoever with viticulture or the breeding of grape varieties expect an answer to the question of whether the stated parentage of the species is correct.

At our present stage of knowledge there is no justification for doubting the parentage which Müller-Thurgau himself indicated for this variety, whether for genetic, or any other reasons. For the time being the great variability of hereditary factors in the parent varieties of the *müller-thurgau* make any final conclusions or doubts inadmissible. Encouraged by the success of the *müller-thurgau* grape variety, my predecessor in Geisenheim, the late Professor Dr Birk, cultivated approximately 30,000 seedlings of the *riesling x silvaner* cross to try to improve on the success of the variety. Müller-Thurgau himself had used only 150 seedlings, but the 30,000 did not produce a single type which surpassed our *müller-thurgau* strain. There can be no better proof of the enormous variability of this vine's hereditary factors. Only three varieties emerged from the 30,000 seedlings: *ehrenfelser*, *osteiner* and *oraniensteiner*; all three pretty closely resemble the *riesling*. Today nobody knows which type of *riesling* Professor Müller-Thurgau used, and the debate over the *müller-thurgau* variety's parentage should be ended once and for all. We really have no choice – now that 100 years have passed – but to accept the statements made about its origin. For the knowledgeable breeder of vines there can be no more doubt.

After all, Müller-Thurgau was the first to produce controlled cross-breeds in Geisenheim. Before he came on the scene cross-breeding was done on a hit and miss basis, without castration. The French even advised the use of several paternal species for pollination. Most data concerning the parents of such varieties could therefore be no more than inspired guess work. Müller-Thurgau had studied the biology of the vine blossom in detail before starting his cross-breeding experiments. He made elaborate arrangements to prevent fertilisation from outside. He used unpollinated, castrated blossoms as a control: 'The unpollinated remained alive for weeks, but their fruit bulbs did not grow in size', he said in a letter to Dr Ziegler. In the aforementioned letter, he continued: 'As far as the hybrid *riesling* x *silvaner* I have brought into circulation is concerned, the *riesling*, as you correctly presume [the white, cultivated in the Rheingau], is the mother, the green *silvaner* the father vine . . . nevertheless, I had cuttings from my earlier breeds sent here and my friend, HW Dahlem, the general secretary of the German viticultural society, who lived in Geisenheim at the time, was kind enough to cut the shoots according to my chart and send them here carefully labelled and packed.'

No other grape variety has achieved such rapid distribution in only a few decades, and no other has been fought over as passionately as the *müller-thurgau* – the first new grape variety to have been produced at a scientific research institute. Vintners and wine lovers decided in favour of the *müller-thurgau* in the end. Only fifty years ago its opponents wanted it banned; today their voices are less strident, but they have not yet been completely silenced. Georg Scheu was one of the promoters of the *müller-thurgau* vine. He had the vision to see that the variety would go a long way!

Müller-Thurgau wines are elegant, palatable, harmonious and mild. Riesling drinkers sometimes find them too mild. They may have a muscat-like bouquet, determined in part by soil and climate. The wine develops rapidly wherever it is grown and should be drunk when still young. It is digestible, fresh, lively, invigorating and light. Such a wine is popular and satisfies the needs of our modern times. In Germany its neutral character ensures a wide selection of bottled wines, from very dry via medium and mild of QbA level to Kabinett, Spätlese and the great Auslese, Beerenauslese and Trockenbeerenauslese wines.

Today *müller-thurgau* is the most important grape variety in German

The Rhine gorge at Assmannshausen with its west-facing vineyards.

viticulture. This was not always so. Sixty-five years ago *müller-thurgau* was being cultivated in Germany on just four hectares; now there are 24,000 hectares. Distribution varies: Franken, Rheinhessen and Baden have a very large share, followed by Rheinpfalz and Nahe. The classic *riesling* areas have the smallest share, for instance, the Rheingau; but the size of the cultivation area is not the only factor in assessing the importance of this grape variety. Some wine-growing regions bring more than a half of their vintage onto the market as Müller-Thurgau wine. Today the Müller-Thurgau is so much a part of our wine range that all serious experts regard it as a 'typically German' variety. The *müller-thurgau* underlines the fact that next to the traditional grape varieties new, efficient breeds are very much needed in our northern climate; were it otherwise, the *müller-thurgau* would not have survived in the face of so much official and professional hostility.

Georg Scheu was another eponymous creator of a grape variety. Scheu was no doctor, no professor, but he was a graduate of Geisenheim and had enormous knowledge of grapes, vines and wines. From his work as a viticultural teacher in the Rheinhessen wine area of Germany, a job which he did for many decades, he knew the problems of the growers in this region, which had been dominated mainly by the *silvaner* grape for a long time. As a student at Geisenheim, Scheu had admired the Rheingau rieslings, so he became involved in clonal selection and vine improvement based on what he had learnt at Geisenheim. However, it was not possible for him to achieve improved ripeness of the *riesling* or a better bouquet for *silvaner*.

Gewürztraminer was always a lazy variety with either low or no yield in those days, so Scheu started to cross-breed. It fascinated him to apply Mendelian laws to viticulture and in 1915 he crossed *silvaner* (as a mother vine) with *riesling* (as a father vine). *Scheurebe* is *silvaner* x *riesling* and *müller-thurgau riesling* x *silvaner*. From the seedlings, No 88 was raised in 1916 in Alzey. His aim was to obtain a better *silvaner* with more bouquet and frost resistance. Seedling 88, or 'S88' as the growers called it, became one of the most interesting German varieties. In 1956 it was patented under the name *scheurebe* (*rebe* = vine). In 1964 only 342 hectares were planted with *scheurebe*, in 1970 over 1,165 hectares, and in 1973 up to 2,092 hectares. Today, there are more than 4,400 hectares of *scheurebe* in Germany.

It is one of the curiosities of German history that the *scheurebe* is the only grape variety to be 'denazified'. In Hitler's time, the grape acquired the name of a top Nazi official. This name was subsequently dropped and the *scheurebe* now honours one of the greatest grape breeders of our time. Scheu developed a series of new varieties and did a lot to improve viticulture in general. He founded the vine-breeding centre at Alzey, Rheinhessen, which still operates successfully.

What, then, is the reason for this widespread distribution of the *scheurebe* grape? It is one of the most appreciated 'new' varieties in Germany and in some other countries too. The vine itself is strong with dark leaves, and remains active long into autumn. Assimilation takes place late in the year and provides high quality grapes. It grows well in limestone soils, which are common in Rheinhessen and other areas. No chlorosis occurs; indeed, resistance to chlorosis was one of Scheu's objectives. The grapes ripen just before those of the *riesling*. *Schreube* requires good sites to achieve good quality, a fact well known to today's growers. The portion of *prädikatsweins* of *scheurebe* is quite high.

Opposite
Doctor Müller-Thurgau became an honourable member of the German Viticultural Association in 1890.

There are all categories of quality of *scheurebe* – from QbA through Kabinett, Spätlese, Auslese and even to Trockenbeerenauslese dessert quality. Most wines show a fruity style with body, nice acidity and freshness as well. Most impressive is their unmistakable bouquet, typical of this variety only. Some of the matured wines are reminiscent of the smell of fresh fruit and flowers – a *scheubouquet* in Germany, which has become part of modern wine language. Auslese types are discreet and reluctant in their expression of the '*scheu*-character', the wines being closer to riesling. Edelfäule or 'noble rot' improves both these wines. The wines from grapes grown on stony soils are more elegant, those from the heavier lime soils develop more body.

Scheurebe wines have provided a real expansion of experience for the German wine palate and this 'new variety' is well integrated into and has enriched the German range.

The success of Müller-Thurgau and Scheu, and the fact that the ideas of these great personalities are still being followed today, can only act as a stimulus to other German wine growers.

LES TROIS GLORIEUSES

Jean Francois Bazin

The *Trois Glorieuses* are wine or vineyard festivals which take place in Burgundy during the third weekend in November and consist of three events: a chapter of the Confrérie des Chevaliers du Tastevin on the Saturday, followed by the Hospices de Beaune wine sale on the Sunday and, finally, the Paulée de Meursault on the Monday. In Burgundy a real weekend lasts for three full days, finishing on Monday night. This is known locally as a 'revenez-y' ... The *Trois Glorieuses* were originally four in number, but then so were Alexander Dumas' Three Musketeers.

Their conception is due to Georges Rozet, who was one of the founder members of the Confrérie des Chevaliers du Tastevin. Beaune and Meursault already ran twin festivals when, in 1933, Nuits-Saint-Georges conceived the idea of a Nuits wine day. The following year, still at Nuits-Saint-Georges, the Confrérie was born. Thus these two Nuits events came to be associated with those of Beaune and Meursault, though since 1933 the formula has been simplified to the *Trois Glorieuses*: Nuits-Saint-Georges, Beaune and Meursault. The Confrérie has been based at the Château du Clos de Vougeot since 1945, with the result that the latter has been known as Clos de Vougeot, Beaune and Meursault ever since.

The image of the *Trois Glorieuses* is part of France's history going back to the three revolutionary days of the 27, 28 and 29 July, 1830, which saw the departure of Charles X and the arrival of Louis-Philippe.

Thanks to the interest in the young Confrérie shown by the Parisian press the Burgundian *Trois Glorieuses* soon came to be talked about. Once it was definitively established, others followed suit, such as the spring *Trois Glorieuses* comprising the Caveau de Dionysios at Morey-Saint-Denis on Friday, the Tastevinage at the Clos de Vougeot on Saturday and the Hospices des Nuits wine sale on Sunday.

The Hospices des Nuits sale, on the third Sunday of November, is now the largest charity sale in the world. Founded in 1443 by Nicolas Rolin, Chancelier de Bourgogne, the Hôtel-Dieu de Beaune rapidly began to receive a number of donations. In 1645 the Hospice de la Charité was also set up in Beaune, and the two establishments combined in 1805 to form what is now the Hospices de Beaune.

The present estate of this hospice, which is the largest domaine in the region, comprises 550 hectares of fields and arable land, about ten farms, twenty dwelling places, market gardens and … some fifty-three hectares of fine vineyards. Twenty-one viticulturists are employed by the Hospices to run this prestigious vineyard (sufficient in Burgundy to earn the *brevet de noblesse*). The vineyards are all located in Côte de Beaune except for one and a half hectares of Mazis-Chambertin donated in 1977.

For several centuries the Hospices' wines were sold by private contract. Subsequently they were sold by public tender, with posters advertising the sale to the region's wine traders. But business deteriorated in the middle of the last century and the cellars were filled by 953 casks from the years 1847, 1848 and 1849 (one cask contains 228 litres). It was then that Joseph Pétasse took up his pilgrim's staff and took to the road. For two years he travelled abroad selling this stock, and on his return he was able to say to amazed administrators: 'This year you can resume public auctions. The customers are there, our wine is known and appreciated and the buyers will come to us. You will see.' Resume public auctions? True, it had been tried in the past, but without success.

This was in 1851. It was not until 1859 that public auctioning was established irrevocably. Since then it failed to take place in 1910 because of the total lack of harvest, was deferred in 1916, suspended from 1939 to 1942, and has sometimes been cancelled because of the mediocre quality of the harvest and replaced by sale through sealed tender (1956 and 1968, for example).

The sale has been held on a fixed date since 1924, when it was linked to the recently created Gastronomic Fair at Dijon. Since 1959 it has been conducted at the wine market near the Hôtel-Dieu. Before 1925 it occupied the main courtyard of the Hôtel-Dieu and the Chambre du Roi and from 1925 to 1959 it took place in the Hospices fermenting room.

It is always presided over by a public figure: Prince Bernhardt of the Netherlands (1954), Archduke Otto of Hapsburg (1964), Prince Henry and Princess Margrethe of Denmark (1971), the Duke of Kent (1973), or an ambassador, a famous musician, an actor, a Nobel Prize winner … etc.

Since 1931 the sale has been run by an official valuer. Previously the Mayor of Beaune himself conducted the auction, using the procedure based on the extinguishing of candles. The Mayor's participation was strictly illegal, being in violation of a law passed during the Revolution which is still in force. The official valuer has sole right to the running of public auctions in France. Recently (1970), the Beaune wine brokers contested this privilege, but the court ruled in favour of the official valuer and he still wields the fateful hammer.

Opposite
The Gothic courtyard of the Hôtel-Dieu in Beaune with its roofs of polychrome tiles.

Above and opposite Tasting
wine in the cellars of the
Hospices.

Auction by candle

'Second and last candle…'

'Second and last candle, ladies and gentlemen. We have 12,500 here on the
left. A last little effort, please!'

Would the Patriarchal House, usually the leader, follow on this occasion?
The whole room held its breath…

The ancient tradition of auction by candle still survives. The vats, each
bearing the names of donors (Guigone de Salins, Docteur Peste, Charlotte
Dumay, etc.) are put up for sale lot by lot following the order given in the
catalogue. They have already been tasted, either the day before or the
same morning, in the Hospices cellars. The wines are, of course, still in
their infancy.

Bidding starts from a reserve price fixed in advance by the directors. At
the first bid a candle is lit which is called the 'first flame'. When this candle
is about to go out and if the bidding is going well, the official valuer lights a
second candle, followed by a third and so on. This is still the continuation

of the 'first flame', which goes on for as long as the bids continue to rise.

When they begin to slow down, the official valuer lights a 'second flame', whose extinction completes the sale. Actually the official valuer carries on lighting candles throughout as long as the bids keep coming, the distinction between the first and second flame being in reality merely decorative.

The auction lasts all afternoon, alternating between slack periods and startling 'heart stoppers'. Of course the Burgundian wine Gotha is there in the room. The purchases are for the most part made by groups, and the buyer publicly links the names of his principal foreign clients to his successful bid. These will include well known importers, restaurant and hotel owners, whose names are thus displayed in this dazzling honours list. As at all great auctions, extremely business-like men are to be seen alongside devastatingly elegant women.

Being a charity sale is does not provide an accurate yardstick of the state of the Burgundian viticultural economy. The prices operated here are very noticeably higher than those on the open market. But the Beaune sale encourages business and, with a world-wide impact, spreads the image of the vintage abroad.

The quantity varies a great deal: less than 300 casks in 1965, more than

The auction *à la chandelle*.

700 in 1982. Total receipts have risen considerably, from one to two million francs in the sixties to nearly ten million francs in 1979 and over twelve million francs in 1982. The average cask price then reached 17,169 francs for 300 bottles. Records are between 120,000 and 150,000 francs per cask, depending on whether it was for a 'peacock tail' vat, or a cask sold by the president, the profit of which was assigned to some charitable or communal cause. On that day the wine goes to Beaune's head and its spirit rejoices.

Paulée de Meursault

If the wine sale of the Hospices de Beaune dates from 1859, the Paulée de Meursault is of more recent origin.

In Burgundy, a *paulée* is a sort of meal or snack marking the end of the harvest. The custom is for the head of the vineyard to invite all the vintagers to his table (either in his home or al fresco) for a communal celebration of the family's latest birth: that of the new wine. In certain villages this is known as the 'dog-killing'. No one knows why, the secret is lost in the mists of time.

Meursault, the temple of the great white wines, had its *paulée*. In 1932, Comte Jules Lafon (1864-1940) had the idea of assembling the entire village for a meal to which each landowner or viticulturist would bring one or

Opposite
The auction in the wine market at Beaune.

.more bottles from his personal cache. Each was to pass from one to another in a spirit of the utmost friendliness.

Comte Lafon, an old man of Socratic countenance and Horatian spirit, invented a literary prize to enliven the festival. It was originally awarded to writers in whose work Burgundy was celebrated (Gaston Roupnel, Raymond Dumay, Colette, Marie Noël, Jacques de Lacretelle, Francis Ambrière, Henri Vincenot) before eligibility for it was extended. The tradition was interrupted in 1938, but resumed in 1950, recipients of the Paulée de Meursault prize including, among many others, Maurice Druon, Paul Guth, Paul Vialar, Harry Yoxall, Hervé Bazin, André Roussin and Jean d'Ormesson. The prize, which was originally provided by Comte Lafon, consisted of 300 bottles of Meursault. Today it is 100 bottles, which the viticulturists of the community take in turns to donate. This meal, unique to Burgundy, begins at about midday and finishes … when it is time for dinner.

Confrérie des Chevaliers du Tastevin

Among those things one has to have done are to have been to La Scala or the Bolshoi, seen the Pyramids illuminated by the setting sun, climbed the Eiffel Tower, seen the Buddha at Nara, lingered for a moment on the lawn before the Capitol in Washington, dreamt, been in love in Delphi, in

The dinner at the Clos de Vougeot is a happy combination of the best wines in Burgundy with the richness of the gastronomy.

Opposite
Clos de Vougeot where over one hundred acres are contained within the single wall built seven hundred years ago.

The 'extremely business-like men and devastatingly elegant women' relax after the auction.

Opposite
The singing of the Cadets of Bourgogne is one of the highspots of the dinner.

Florence … But one absolutely must have participated at least once in one's life in a Chapter of the Confrérie des Chevaliers du Tastevin.

Born on 16 November, 1934 at Nuits-Saint-Georges, and subsequently welcomed to the Clos de Vougeot (the old wine district of the Citeaux monks), the Confrérie represents for Burgundy, as Lucien Boitouzet puts it, 'what the Comédie Française and the Légion d'honneur together represent for France'. The Tastevin was created by Camille Rodier (1890-1963) and George Faiveley (1887-1968) in response to the viticultural crisis of the

The vineyards of the Clos
de Vougeot.

thirties. The idea can be expressed in a handful of words: 'Since nobody wants our wines, why not invite our friends to come and drink it with us?', thereby inventing public relations.

A feast, no doubt, but not just a feast. A Chapter effects a happy combination of the best wines in Burgundy with the richness of its gastronomy, the singing of the Cadets de Bourgogne with the conversation of the Confrérie's dignitaries, culminating in the high point of the evening: the enthronement. Inspired by Rabelais and Molière, postulant knights of the brotherhood are invited to penetrate Circles of wine to accede to that signal honour, the right to don the purple and gold ribbon of the Confrérie.

> 'By Noah, father of the vine,
> By Bacchus, god of wine,
> By Saint Vincent, patron saint of vine growers,
> We dub you Chevalier du Tastevin.'

The silver tastevin which decorates this ribbon is the tool of the viticulturists' trade and is indispensable in wine testing. Respected as a precious object it should never be used as, say, an ash tray, on pain of complete loss of respect in Burgundy!

The Chapter of the *Trois Glorieuses* is one of seventeen annual Chapters (Renoweau, Tulipes, Feuillaison, Roses, Vendanges, Sarments, etc.). The Confrérie des Chevaliers du Tastevin is the oldest and most famous of all the wine brotherhoods. Fifty years after its foundation, and still just as young, it expresses certain 'true truths'. Wine is a universal language, an Esperanto for the fraternity. Humour, wit, tact, and a sense of proportion are elements in this chemistry, for the Tastevin places wine at the service of the genuine values of civilisation. One raises one's glass, to be sure, but not solely for the pleasure of emptying it. Rather, we see here the Burgundian face of humanism.

The world comes to the Clos de Vougeot, but what do they expect to find there? 'Something greater than wine, for wine itself is greater than wine', replies Raymond Dumay. 'It is the mysterious virtue of the Confrérie which it would be as futile to try to analyse as it would be to dare to stroke a butterfly's wings.'

Since 1934, some 18,000 postulants have penetrated the Circles of wine, swearing fealty to the wine of France and to that of Burgundy in particular, adopting the motto: *'Jamais en vain toujours en vin.'*

Instituted in 1939, the Commanderie d'Amerique in the United States numbers today 1,900 members distributed among thirty-three sub-commanderies. Other commanderies exist in Morocco, Senegal, the Ivory Coast, the Bermudas, Australia and so on. Thus Gaston Roupnel's vow has been fulfilled, for he dreamt that one day he would see 'the world toast France's health in Burgundy's wine'.

WATCH OUT FOR THESE WINES

Oz Clarke

That's the great thing about living in London. When your editor tells you to take a trip round the whole world of wine – east to west, north to south – you don't have to dash off to Airey & Neave for your tropical kit, Thomas Cook for your Superpex Economy return and Saint Pancras Hospital for your jabs. No; you just sit and wait. Over any twelve-month period the world of wine will come to *you*, because the British market is the one everybody longs to crack, and London is the centre of that market.

So when I started thinking about what vinous globetrotting I *might* engage in during the forthcoming year, I realised it was a far more practical idea to pick out the wines of the world which had come to me in the last few months; and I couldn't have tasted a wider variety if I'd been Phineas Fogg, Doctor Livingstone and Marco Polo all improbably rolled into one.

France is so close, though, that I wondered if I should miss it out. Miss out France? Never! Perhaps I would miss out Pauillac and Puligny-Montrachet, Champagne and Chablis, because others will do their wines more justice than I can, but I wouldn't miss out France any more than I would eat my smoked salmon with sliced white bread and margerine.

As a compromise, I shall miss out the famous bits, which does mean that I won't spend much time in Champagne, Bordeaux and Burgundy. Even so, I shall snoop round the edges, and Burgundy is where I shall start. Chablis is by turns famous and infamous for its sometimes steely, always dry, whites, affordable or impossibly overpriced, depending upon the whim of the weather and the producer. The *chardonnay* grape makes Chablis, but if you take the road out west from the town itself, there's an area round Saint Bris which grows all the wrong grapes on the wrong side of the tracks yet the wine is never overpriced and is always delicious. *Aligoté* and *sauvignon* are the two white grapes, and while the Aligoté is excellently fresh, the buttermilk nose blending with a strong, dry, appley

The village and vineyards of St Bris near Chablis.

fruit, the Sauvignon de Saint Bris is quite simply one of France's best, very dry, and bursting with tangy gooseberry and asparagus fruit which makes me remember wistfully that Sancerre once tasted like that too. They make red wine as well, from the *pinot noir*, and at a time when good, affordable red burgundy is an endangered species, this is light, strawberryish in taste, and first rate value for money. My favourite producers are Brocard and Pinon for whites and Brocard (again), Bienvenue and Defrance for reds.

It really pains me to have to dash past Beaujolais this year, with so many of the wonderful '85s now ready to drink, but I'm off to the Rhône valley for my next stop. Well, off to *off* the Rhône valley – the Ardèche to be exact. This is my sort of paradise – high, tangling hills, thick with forest and split by streams and gorges way up to the west of the Rhône valley floor. You'll have seen these beckoning beguilingly to your right as you sweat and curse your way south along the autoroute. This time, turn off for a moment – up into the rare, quiet air of these hills, and find some of the richest, juiciest (and cheapest) Gamay in all of France, sturdy dark Syrah, gulping fresh Grenache rosé and disconcertingly serious Chardonnay, all at featherlight prices from the local co-ops, UCCA, UCOVA and Saint Désirat-Champagne.

So, let's go from one wild paradise to a dusty, rockstrewn wilderness on the back road from Avignon to Arles – the Côteaux des Baux. There seems to be no earth, nowhere flat or symmetrical – surely nothing can grow here – but, by God, vines can, with *cabernet* and *syrah* combining miraculously to produce some of the most exciting blackcurrant and raspberry-sweet reds I've ever tasted. The out-and-out star is Domaine de Trévallon, but Terres Blanches and Mas de Gourgonnier are wonderful too.

I really must move on from France, but a last optimistic lunge to the west and north will unearth two more forgotten jewels before I go. Gaillac has become so closely identified with boringly dry reds and whites, usually in a bag-in-box, that the area's potential has been submerged in mediocrity. Enter Jean Cros, a Gaillacois who won't let his traditions die. His red is so peppery and sharply fruity that it makes you want to catch your breath, but take a second sip and marvel at the austere, shocking proudness of the wine. If you're still unconvinced, he makes a traditional sparkling wine too, a heavenly blend of peach, apple, pear – and tobacco (!) – flavours. These are two of France's most individual wines.

I've only my last Loire jewel to reveal. Hemmed in by the fields and meadows south of Saumur are the remains of the once-flourishing vineyards of Thouarsais. Could wines this good really become extinct? Only one man stands between Thouarsais and extinction – Monsieur Gigon. His white Chenin is so brilliantly green – biting, refreshing and warming all at once – and his Cabernet has all the earthy green-peppery character one fears in Anjou, but which here is joined with a delicate fruit

which is almost absurdly ripe and sweet, that as long as *he* keeps going, Thouarsais will keep going too.

I knew I should have resisted the temptations of France, because I could spend ages more sniffing out her hidden genius; but now it's over the Alps and into Italy. The Sudtirol is Italian by decree, but not by nature. They *will* speak Italian to you, but they speak German by choice, and this breathtakingly beautiful valley, towered over by the Dolomite peaks, was Austria's southernmost province till Italy 'acquired' it in 1919 as a 'thank you' for making the right noises during the First World War.

The wines are similarly un-Italian using the whole gamut of French and German grape varieties, as well as one or two local specialities. Already they are producing Italy's best Chardonnay – sharp, sometimes slightly prickly, but with lemon intensity, backed up as the wine ages by creamy softness. And it does age. I've had twenty-year-old Pinot Biancos and Chardonnays which were deep, golden and toffee-rich. Gewürztraminer probably originated in the local village of Tramin, and though the wines are fairly light – crops are very big here – yet a few years' age brings out all the exotic lychee fragrance but none of the oily excess of Alsace's top examples. And another Alsace lookalike which gets fresh treatment is the Muscat, here usually called the Goldmuskateller. Ideally made dry, it has all the

MARQUES DE GRIÑON

Gran vino blanco seco

DENOMINACION DE ORIGEN

RUEDA SUPERIOR

1983

Embotellado por

Bodega de Crianza, Castilla la Vieja S.A.

(Rueda, Valladolid)

75 cl

PRODUCE OF SPAIN   12,5% vol.

RE 5693 VA   RS 302478 VA

№ 027989

crunchy green juiciness of a fistful of fresh grapes guzzled in the heat of high summer.

Sudtirol reds are just as exciting, and again are marked by piercing flavours when young, ageing to a soft balanced beauty over anything from five to twenty years. Cabernet is all fire and earth to start, but, given time, blends the grassy acidity with gentle blackcurrant fruit, and is like nothing so much as one of those ageless delights of the Loire – Bourgueil or Chinon. Pinot Noir certainly starts out light, but the plum, raspberry and cherry perfume is enough to fill a room. It, too, ages to a sweet maturity, lacking only the dangerous rotty richness of great burgundy. And then there's Lagrein. This is one of those untraceable local grapes Italy is full of, and while it usually makes Italy's best rosé, it's the red I love. Opaque purple for years, finally turning to a deep smoky blood red, such wine should by rights taste harsh and tannic in the Italian mould – but it doesn't. Right from the start it's packed with chocolate and plum sweetness, licorice even, with a streak of pine resin and herbs. It's big, yes – it's sometimes enormous – but right through its twenty-year life span soft enough to smile over.

I suppose I'm so fond of good Rioja that I've been less adventurous in exploring Spain than most countries, preferring to stick with the gentle vanilla-like reds of Caceres, El Coto, Lancorta and Montecillo. But once again, Spain came to town in a big way this year, and on my *next* trip there I'll be heading off the beaten track as soon as I've left the airport. And I'll make for Catalonia, not for its sparkling wines, nor even for its big oaky reds, but for one of the world's best and most under-rated Rieslings – the

Waltraud Riesling of Torres. Maybe you should expect Miguel Torres, one of the world's greatest wine makers, to produce one of the world's great rieslings. But in Spain? Somehow he's preserved all the blade-running steeliness of the grape, and yet drawn out a full, soft fruit; very dry but wonderfully refreshing. I've never been able to find anyone who actually stocks the wine, so maybe the Torres family have the good sense to drink it all themselves.

Catalonia is more famous for its reds, usually grown near the coast. But one of her best comes from the parched flat hinterland between Barcelona and Zaragoza where a member of the family which makes Codorniu sparkling wine has set up house at the castle of Raimat. Like the good Catalan he is, he planted a vineyard and the result is Raimat Abadia, a mix of Cabernet and Tempranillo which is so delicate, so fragrant and so bursting with juicy, blackcurrant fruit that I couldn't decide whether it reminded me more of the classical balance of Bordeaux or the unbridled self-confidence of Australia. Which in my language are two pretty big compliments to pay a wine.

But then, in a particularly anonymous part of central Spain near Madrid, called Malpica de Tajo, there's a Cabernet Sauvignon being made which is so intense, the fumes of blackcurrant and cedar seeming to rise in the glass from the very heart of the wine, that you'd think it had to be a classed growth Bordeaux – until you saw the price and realised you were saving yourself at least £100 a case on wine of this quality. It's called Marqués de Griñon, and, well, the consultants do just happen to be Alexis Lichine and Professor Emile Peynaud – which is about as 'classed growth claret' as you can get.

I'll skirt across the north-western tip of Iberia, pausing just long enough to knock back an ice cold mug of the excellent Galician white Pazo del Ribeiro; I'll ford the Minho river, and find myself in the thick of one of Europe's most original wine countries – Portugal. Vinho Verde is a completely under-rated wine style, since it is usually sweetened and softened for export, but the 'real thing' is a sensation, being incredibly, and I mean *incredibly*, dry, yet packed with peppery, grapefruity flavour, apricot sometimes, peaches even, and topped off with the tiniest of sparkles. A fine single estate wine like Solar de Bourcas makes a mockery of the stuff we normally see.

If Vinho Verde is an ideal hot weather white, Portugal's most fascinating wines are mostly red, and many of the flavours are rewardingly un-French. The hills round Tras os Montes have spent most of the last forty years churning out Mateus Rosé, but the locals prefer to drink red, and I choose the almost absurdly soft Unamontes which has a gentle candy spice flavour that is quite lovely. I could then stumble down the valley to find some more surprises. The Douro river is always thought of as the 'port' river, but they make loads of table wine too. Reds are best, and they develop a toffee softness as they age, a slight whiff of tobacco and pepper and an unexpected gentle raspberry fruit pastille sweetness. They're a bit like Cahors decked out in their Sunday best, and my favourite is the Caves Acacio 1978 Reserva.

The Portuguese area to make the greatest impact recently has been Bairrada – a rather scrubby, sandy seaside area, not pretty to look at but producing a wine which is the essence of perfumey blackcurrants. It retains some toughness for a long time, but the fruit is so thrilling that the tannin

and acidity seem, if anything, to accentuate it. All impecunious claret lovers should get on the first plane to Oporto and head south to firms like Saõ Jaõ (the best), Acacio and Cantanhede, and start by drinking the 1978, but be prepared to head back twenty years or more.

If I'd headed back twenty years in New Zealand, the chances of finding something decent of any colour would have been close to zero, but the social and wine-making revolution which has transformed Australia into one of the world's most exciting wine producers is now in full, glorious flight in New Zealand as well. Adrift in the southern Pacific swell, New Zealand balances powerful sun with strong westerly winds and a daily ritual of white rain clouds gathering round her mountain peaks. Heat, breeze and rainfall – a perfect vineyard recipe.

It's the whites which so far shine. One taste of Selaks gooseberry-sharp, shockingly full-fruited Sauvignon 1985 will snap your eyes open. A taste of

the Matua Valley Yates Estate Chardonnay 1985, soft and ripe, and full of
Côte d'Or 'dry lusciousness', coated with the coffee beans and toast
savouriness of new oak, makes you wonder why you bother with
Puligny-Montrachet at three times the price. Mission Vineyards produce
the kind of tangy, lemon and asparagus, yet honey-edged Semillon/
Sauvignon which would make a Graves producer weep. The guys in Alsace
would be weeping too if they ever deigned to taste the Matawhero
Gewürztraminer from Gisborne, its peppery oiliness effortlessly matched
by the peachy fruit and dry, spicy perfume. And at Canterbury on the
South Island, they might even achieve the impossible and make a
Burgundian weep. Saint Helena produces a Pinot Noir which is so fragrant,
so packed with cherry and strawberry sweetness but just beginning to
show the sultry smoky brilliance, the plum-rotty danger of great Burgundy,
that if I owned a few acres in Gevrey Chambertin, I'd spend my next
summer hols in New Zealand trying to work out how they do it.

So to Australia. Where to start is the problem here. There's no country in
the world so intent on producing an endless array of brilliant flavours, new
producers and new areas shouting their arrival with every vintage. I'll
begin in the west and try not to dally. The quality of black grapes grown
south of Perth is so remarkable that I can effortlessly choose three totally
different styles. Peel Estate makes a stingingly intense Shiraz, all pepper
and fire like a young Hermitage, but brought quickly into line with a gentle
raspberry depth of sweetness. Cape Mentelle produces a Zinfandel,

poached from California, within spitting distance of the Indian Ocean. It's one of the best Zins I have ever tasted. And Mosswood, ah Mosswood. Cabernets, Pinot Noirs, Semillons and Chardonnays of quite breathtaking quality, Burgundy's and Bordeaux's brilliance combined on the backwoods slopes of the Margaret River.

I'm headed for Victoria now, but I'll stop briefly at Adelaide in South Australia to catch my breath. Firstly at Penfolds, where, despite the brutal asset-stripping obsession of their new owners, a new great wine has arisen from what is left of the original Grange Hermitage vineyards at Magill, after the property developers have done their worst. It's called Magill Estate Shiraz, and the 1983 is almost too much of a good thing for a chap to take standing up. The richness, the weight, the ripe intensity of the blackcurrant fruit is almost painful. But what pain. And what great wine it'll be in one, two and three decades' time. And I must call in at the Petaluma Winery in the cloud-high Adelaide Hills. The estate vineyards are still young here, scampering rather sparsely up slopes and down gulleys, but the wine making is in the hands of one of the all-time greats – Brian Croser. The steely brilliance of his Rhine Riesling 1984 from low-yielding Clare Valley vines, and the startling blackcurrant and bramble depth of his Coonawarra Cabernet 1984 (mixed in with a little Merlot) indicates another star glistening in the southern firmament.

It's last stop Victoria, if only because the endless variety of vineyard sites and wine-making possibilities beats that of any other state. I'll start at Delatite in the cool snowy Mansfield Hills way over to the north-east of Melbourne. I could choose the Pinot Noir, the Rhine Riesling or the Gewürztraminer, all remarkable award-winning wines, but I think I'll put my money on the 1984 Cabernet and the 1985 Cabernet-Merlot, brilliant blends of blackcurrant richness and minty fragrance. Above all, the wines are so soft, yet so structured, so brilliant young, so brilliant old, that I've not come across any quite like them before.

Cutting back towards the Western Highlands, I'll stop on the Warrack-Buangor road at Mount Langhi-Giran, where Fratins produce classic reds. The Cabernets are dark, sweet-fruited, blackcurrant- and mint-scented wines for the long haul, while the Shiraz is all pepper and plums and wonderfully unashamed burly fruit. And if I have to finish, I'll make the long treck up to the baking prairie lands of north-east Victoria, and amidst the shacks and sheds of a long-gone era I'll end up at Bailey's, or Chambers, or Stanton and Killeen and wander between the old crabby casks half hidden in the gloom, but full of liqueur muscat lazily ageing to a peak of sweetness, velvety richness, and concentrated grapey fruit so that it's hardly necessary to do more than anoint your lips and the flavour will spread and fill your mouth, and the fumes will fuddle your brain with pleasure.

CONTRIBUTORS

Burton Anderson eight years ago abruptly terminated his career as a 'legitimate journalist' (dealing with such tedious topics as war, crime and politics at the *International Herald Tribune* in Paris) to wander into the miscellaneous world of Italian wine as a writer with no credentials whatsoever. His books *Vino, The Pocket Guide to Italian Wines* and *Burton Anderson's Guide to Italian Wines*, plus hundreds of articles, have given him a degree of credibility and the opportunity to live with his wife and two children at a place called Oliveto in Tuscany, far from the icy winds of his native Minnesota.

John Arlott was born in Basingstoke in 1914 when it was a small country town. By optimism and luck he struggled through work in a town planning office, in a mental hospital and police force to find himself, to his absolute astonishment, working in the three things that delighted him most – association football, when it was a decent game, cricket, and wine – and contriving to remain solvent. He is married with two sons, who drink regularly. He is the author of *Burgundy Vines and Wines* (with Christopher Fielden); *Krug, House of Champagne*; and *Arlott on Wine* (edited by David Rayvern Allen).

Gerald Asher was educated in England and trained in the wine trade in France, Spain and Germany. He lives in San Francisco, California, where he is chairman of the Mosswood Wine Company (McKesson Corp), and lectures, when he has time, on the wine marketing programme of the University of San Francisco; he also writes a regular 'Wine Journal' for *Gourmet* magazine of New York. He has contributed to a number of books, most recently the University of California's *Book of Wine*, and has published a collection of essays, *On Wine*. He was the 1984 recipient of *Wines and Vines* perpetual award for Excellence in Wine Writing, though he has yet to discover in what way wine writing is supposed to be different from merely writing about wine.

Jean-Francois Bazin Burgundian journalist and writer, was born in Dijon in 1942. He is author of several books, particularly on the wines of France and those of the United States. One of his books, *Dijon, le Temps de Vivre*, won the literary prize of the Confrérie des Chevaliers du Tastevin. Holding a doctorate in law and a diploma from the Institute of Political Studies in Paris, he is also assistant to the Mayor of Dijon, responsible for urban development and open land, and first vice-president of the Burgundian Regional Council, responsible for finance and planning.

Dr Helmut Becker was born in 1927 between grapes and wines at Geisenheim in the heart of the Rheingau. Since 1964 he has been the head of the famous Geisenheim Research Centre which specialises in the development of vines and breeding grapes. He also works closely with the Freiburg Wine Institute and Neustadt Research Centre. Professor Becker's thesis for his doctorate at the University of Mainz was *The Physiology of Phylloxera*. He has written many books, and lectures on viticulture at Bonn University and the German Wine Academy. As a consultant he has travelled in most wine-growing countries, and in 1971 was guest scientist in Australia for three months.

Brian Beet despite a good education and a sound career, has always been an inveterate collector. Starting with stamps, he progressed in maturity through an unfortunate affection for wine, to an obsession with drinking antiques. As his collecting quickly outstretched his income, he gave up respectable employment to become an antique dealer. This allowed him much greater scope to pursue his interests, which rapidly expanded to other areas and, as he says himself, certainly beat working for a living. At present, he is happily ensconced at his shop in Burlington Gardens, opposite the Museum of Mankind.

Michael Broadbent a Mancunian, though best known for his professional wine activities – tasting, auctioning and writing – has other strings to his bow, being an accomplished pianist and artist – an exhibitor at London's Royal Academy, occasional illustrator and currently chairman of the Wine Trade Art Society whose annual exhibition is held at Christie's. He is founder and editor-in-chief of Christie's Wine Publications, author of *Wine Tasting*, now in seven languages, and *The Great Vintage Wine Book*. His work in the field of wine has been recognised by the French government who, in 1980, gave him the rank of *Chevalier* in the *Ordre National du Mérite*.

Nathan L. Chroman   a practising attorney in Beverly Hills and the president of the Transportation Commission for the city of Los Angeles, has been the chairman of the Los Angeles County Fair Wine Judging since 1967. He has taught a wine appreciation course since 1959 at the University of California at Los Angeles, Extension Division. He has also authored the *Treasury of American Wines*, published in 1973 and contributed to the North American section for *Wines of the World*, a revised edition of André Simon's book. Since 1969, Nathan has been a regular, contributing wine columnist to the *Los Angeles Times*, and also on the Times National Syndicate.

Oz Clarke   was awarded the Glenfiddich prize for Wine Writer of the Year in 1983. His first book, *Webster's Wine Price Guide* won the *What Wine?* Book of the Year award in 1984. He is a prolific writer and contributes to national newspapers, wine and glossy magazines. Before turning to writing professionally on wine Oz Clarke was, in 1973, the youngest ever Wine Taster of the Year and, in 1980, Captain of the all-conquering England Wine Tasters. Oz Clark is also a leading West End actor and singer. Recent roles include Perón in *Evita* and Esmond Romilly in *The Mitford Girls*. He also appeared in *Sweeny Todd* and the BBC Shakespeare series. It is perhaps this unusual diversification of interests that brings to his wine writing the zest, clarity and sense of humour for which it has become renowned. He appears regularly on radio and television.

José Ignacio Domecq   is a small intense man, wirey and lean, with a prominent 'nose' made famous by many advertising campaigns. Over 70, he still plays polo, rides every day and sails his 40 foot yacht. His 6000 choice acres of white chalky soil north-west of Jerez have been producing wine since the days of the

Romans and Phoenicians. He has other interests in northern Spain, Mexico, Venezuela and Colombia. His family founded Spain's first polo club and the Spanish Riding School in Jerez, using bloodstock from the original Lipizzaner horses. José Ignacio Domecq, who produces some of the world's finest sherries, arrives each day at his office on an old motor bike with Pico, his beloved Jack Russell terrier, in a basket at the back. He 'does not know the meaning of the word retirement'.

Prince Yuri Galitzine is the great great nephew of one of the legendary figures of the wine industry of imperial Russia, Prince Leon Galitzine, whose vineyards in the Crimea are still a show place in Soviet Russia today. Born after the Revolution, Yuri Galitzine is a keen historian and a gastronome, as a result of which he has always sought to maintain the traditions of his family at the table. His love of wine has perforce developed by a long association with France, where he now owns a farmhouse not far from Bordeaux and where he is also a Commander of the Compagnons de Beaujolais.

James Halliday made his first trip to the vineyards of the Hunter Valley in 1958, marking the start of a lifelong love affair with wine and the wine industry, first becoming a partner in a weekend vineyard in the Hunter Valley, which produces fine wine under the Brokenwood label. Since moving to Victoria, he is no longer a partner in Brokenwood, but made his first Yarra Valley wine in 1985 and looks forward to the day when he will retire from his position as a senior partner of a large law firm and become a full-time *vigneron*, wine writer and wine consultant. He has been a national wine show judge for many years and is a wine consultant, specialising in imported wines, and making regular trips to France. But most importantly he is a wine writer, well known for his weekly columns in the *National Times* and the *Australian*. He is also the author of: *Wine and History of the Hunter Valley* (1979), *Wines and Wineries of New South Wales* (1980), *Wines and Wineries of South Australia* (1981), *Wines and Wineries of Victoria* (1982), *Wines and Wineries of Western Australia* (1982), *Vintage Halliday* (1982), *Coonawarra: The History, the Vignerons and the Wines* (1983), and *Clare Valley: The History, the Vignerons and the Wines* (1985).

Hugh Johnson was a pupil of the late André Simon, first in 1962 as secretary of the Wine & Food Society, then as editor of *Wine & Food*. His first book, *Wine*, published in 1966, is still in print. In 1970 he wrote *The World Atlas of Wine* and each year since 1977 has revised his annual *Pocket Wine Book*. Between whiles he has written books on trees, *The Principles of Gardening*, and continues to conduct *The Garden* (the journal of the RHS) and its sister-magazine *The Plantsman*. In 1983 he published *Hugh Johnson's Wine Companion, an Encyclopedia of Wines, Vineyards and Winemakers*, and in 1984 a video film, *How to Handle a Wine*. He is currently working on a history of wine between weeding and feeding his growing collection of trees.

Michael Kuh is a native New Yorker and photojournalist who has lived in Europe most of his life. Whether as writer, photographer, or both combined, he regularly describes the European wine scene to a worldwide audience, via major magazines and syndication. His friendship with José Ignacio Domecq dates back to 1966, when he covered the Jerez Spring Fair for *Life*. He confesses 'I guess I'm responsible for his fame as "the Nose".

Patrick Leigh Fermor was born in 1915 of English and Irish descent. After a calamitous school career, he lived and travelled in the Balkans and the Greek Archipelago. During that time he acquired a deep interest in languages and a love of remote places. He joined the Irish Guards in 1939, became liaison officer in Albania, and fought in Greece and Crete to which, during the German occupation, he returned three times (once by parachute). Disguised as a shepherd, he lived for over two years in the mountains organizing the resistance and the capture and evacuation of the German Commander. Patrick Leigh Fermor has also written *The Traveller's Tree* about the West Indies, which won the Heinemann Foundation Prize for Literature in 1950 and the Kemsley Prize in 1951, *A Time to Keep Silence, The Violins of Saint Jacques, Roumeli* (Penguin), and *A Time of Gifts* (Penguin).

Simon Loftus erstwhile stilt-walker and magician's stooge, has achieved a measure of respectability as a director of Adnams, the Suffolk brewers. During the last fifteen years he has transformed the company's wine department into one of the most interesting and adventurous wine merchants in the country. His annual catalogue (packed with gossip about the growers and illustrated by his own photographs) has become compulsive reading for wine lovers all over the world. He also writes occasional articles for a variety of magazines (including the trade press) which often infuriate eminent wine men, despite the natural benevolence of the author.

Tall, dark and handsome Simon is married to Irène, beautiful but loopy. They have a daughter whose ambition is to climb Mount Everest with a grand piano.

Patrick Matthews spent most of his working life with Condé Nast Publications, interrupted by war service and ten years making specialised films. He succeeded Harry Yoxall as a director of The International Wine & Food Society and was awarded the silver medal. His first assignment after war service was to start the English edition of *House & Garden*. On his retirement he became a consultant with Mitchell Beazley, edited the second edition of Hugh Johnson's *World Atlas of Wine*, and inspired his *Pocket Wine Book*, which spawned the whole pocket book series. Since 1979 he has been the editor of Christie's Wine Publications. With his wife he has produced over thirty books (sales over a million), and thirteen films for BBC TV, about a teddy bear called Teddy Edward. He takes the photographs himself and, with Teddy Edward, has been to Timbuctoo, Mount Everest and the bottom of the Grand Canyon.

Peter Meltzer was born in possibly the worst vintage year of the post-war era (1951). He overcame this handicap and left his native Canada (where he received an MA in history at Trinity College, University of Toronto) in search of better domestic wines. Today he is a wine writer and restaurant reviewer residing in New York. His work has appeared in the *New York Times, Town & Country, Connoisseur, Food & Wine, Art & Auction* and the *Wine Spectator*. He has also co-authored and published *Passport to New York Restaurants*, a pocket guide.

Edmund Penning-Rowsell is wine correspondent of the *Financial Times* and *Country Life*, and chairman since 1964 of The International Exhibition Co-operative Wine Society. When Christie's restarted regular wine auctions in 1966, he researched the vast collection of Christie's wine catalogues from 1766 onwards. From them he picked out items of interest reflecting the tastes and prices of the time, and these have formed the basis of the market reviews in Christie's Wine Reviews. He is the author of *The Wines of Bordeaux* (5th revised edition, 1986). He has been decorated by the French government as *Chevalier de l'Ordre du Mérite Agricole* (1971) and *Chevalier de l'Ordre National du Mérite* (1981).

Dr Louis Skinner   Lou, as he is affectionately known in the world of food and wine, is a dermatologist who practises in Coral Gables, Florida. In 1962 he founded the Miami branch of the International Wine & Food Society and has long been a prominent member of its North American committee. In 1982 he formed the Miami chapter of the *Commanderie de Bordeaux* and is currently *Maître*. He is *Officier Commandeur* of the Miami chapter of the *Chevaliers de Tastevin* and *Charge de Mission* of the *Chaîne des Rotisseurs* as well as being a member of several wine fraternities in France. It is hardly surprising that he has been awarded the *Medaille d'Honneur* of the *Comité National des Vins de France* and in 1985, the year he was 'Mr Gourmet' of the Bacchus Society, he received official French Government recognition as an *Officier dans l'Ordre du Mérite Agricole*. Above all, he has a profound knowledge of fine food and wine and a generous heart to go with it.

Steven Spurrier   joined the London wine trade in 1964 and left for France in 1968 to avoid sitting the Master of Wine examinations. In 1970 he purchased the Caves de la Madeleine in the centre of Paris, and two years later opened L'Academie du Vin, a wine school which now has branches in many countries, including Chez Christe's in London. He is titular head of the Mafia Anglais in the Paris wine trade, where his other interests include a restaurant, wine bar and a second shop on the left bank, while in London he is a director of the Malmaison Wine Club and the Caves de la Madeleine (UK) Ltd. He has written three and co-authored two books on wine, but has yet to win a prize of any kind.

Serena Sutcliffe   is an international wine consultant and broker and, *par-dessus le marché*, a Master of Wine. Actually, she would prefer to be on a permanent Grand Tour, but lacks Boswell's passion for letter writing and Goethe's prodigious talent. 1986 saw the publication of her *Pocket Guide to the Wines of Burgundy*, which has already been sold in many languages around the world.

Pamela Vandyke Price was the first person outside the wine trade to be allowed to take the examinations prepared for its students, in which she gained four certificates of merit. Winner of the first Glenfiddich Award and Trophy in 1971, she won the Glenfiddich Silver Medal in 1973. In 1979 the *Comité Interprofessionel du Vin de Champagne* bestowed on her their *Diplôme d'Honneur* and in 1981 the French government made her a *Chevalier de l'Ordre du Mérite Agricole*. In 1983 she became the first woman ever to have been elected to the Jurade of St Emilion. She has written 24 books on wines and spirits and has contributed to many trade and consumer publications in the UK and overseas, also broadcasting and lecturing. She is the only person outside the wine trade to speak regularly on the wine courses organised by Christie's.

Auberon Waugh columnist, novelist and writer on wine, is also editor of the *Literary Review*. He was born on November 17th, 1939, eldest son of the late Evelyn Waugh. In addition to being wine correspondent of *Harpers and Queen Magazine*, he manages the Spectator Wine Club. Married with four children, and with homes in Somerset, London and the Languedoc to support, he writes a weekly article on politics and current affairs in the *Spectator*, a weekly article on books in the *Daily Mail*, a fortnightly leader page column on current affairs in the *Sunday Telegraph* as well as his monthly wine articles in *Harpers & Queen* and the *Spectator*. Before becoming a full-time journalist he wrote five novels of which the best are *The Foxglove Saga* (1960) and *Consider the Lilies* (1968). He has also published six other books. His latest, *A Turbulent Decade: Diaries of Auberon Waugh 1976–1985*, was published to enormous acclaim towards the end of 1985 and illustrated by William Rushton. Two further books came out in 1986: *Another Voice*, collected *Spectator* essays, from Sidgwick & Jackson, and *The Entertaining Book*, on wine and food, to which his wife contributes the food section, from Hamish Hamilton.

ACKNOWLEDGEMENTS

I am grateful to the photographers who have supplied illustrations for this new edition of *Christie's Wine Companion*; also to Anne-Marie Ehrlich who did so much picture research for this book. I would also like to thank Michael Kuh, who collaborated with José Ignacio Domecq on his chapter, and produced the photographs for pages 36, 37, 38, 39, 40, 122, 126, 127. We were pleased to find the photographs taken by Patrick Eagar for pages 72, 76, 77, 138, 168, 170, 171, 172, 173, 175, 176, 177, 179, 182. Former contributor Jan Read supplied the shots for pages 65, 69 from his extensive library. The photographs on pages 10, 80, 83, 84, 86, 162/163 came from J. Allan Cash Photographers.

I have included, by kind permission of Lansdowne Press, Sydney, pictures on pages 73, 74 of two contrasting Australian wineries. I thank Eliphot, Aix-en-Provence, for the photographs of Beaumanière (pages 144, 146) and Simon Loftus for the photographs on pages 50, 52.

Michael Busselle took the splendid photographs for our cover and pages 57, 58, 59, 60. I also acknowledge the photographs taken by Hugh Johnson 81, Bryan Peterson 89, 128, Jerry Whitaker 122, the Scottish Tourist Board 129, 130, and Lord Snowdon 135. I merely record that I took the photographs on pages 45, 115, 118, 119, 133, 141, 143 and 174.

David Boss, a friend of Nathan Chroman, sent us the witty drawings for his chapter. Jeremy Roberts supplied the illustrations for pages 102, 103. The painting by Philipe Mercier, page 29, came from the Bridgeman Art Library, and the illustrations for Prince Galitzine's chapter are from the ET Archive 11, 12, 14, 20, 23 and the Novodni Press 18, 19, 25.

Mr Shaw of the Guildhall Library in London produced a copy of *Cheers! Fifty Years of Wine Cartoons, New Yorker* from the Master of Wine library which is stored there. The New Yorker Magazine Inc. have given us permission to reproduce their copyright cartoons on pages 33, 46, 62, which captured the current feeling at the time, now happily in the past. The cartoon on page 98 was drawn by John Leech for *Punch*.

Our thanks are due to Peter Willis, who commissioned Kevin Jackson and Rima Farah to illustrate the Bordeaux château used for our frontispiece. Examples from Charles Mozley's lithographs of Bordeaux châteaux commissioned by Hedges & Butler are shown on pages 139 and 140. John Murray Publishers kindly gave us permission to reproduce the extract from Patrick Leigh Fermor's *Mani*.

Finally I must thank Alison Stanford who has sub-edited all Christie's wine books, and has wrestled with the varied requirements of the wine writers over the years. For those of you who did not see the first edition of the *Wine Companion* I should like to repeat again what my old friend Harry Yoxall once wrote in one of his own books: 'I have never yet read any wine book in which I have not spotted some inconsistencies and indeed errors. It is too much to hope that such will not have crept into this one. For these I apologize in advance, and hope they will prove unimportant'.

Patrick Matthews